The Arab Shakespeare Trilogy

The Arab Shakespeare Trilogy

The Al-Hamlet Summit
Richard III, an Arab Tragedy
The Speaker's Progress

By

SULAYMAN AL BASSAM

Introduced by

PROFESSOR GRAHAM HOLDERNESS

B L O O M S B U R Y
LONDON • NEW DELHI • NEW YORK • SYDNEY

Bloomsbury Methuen Drama

An imprint of Bloomsbury Publishing Plc

50 Bedford Square	1385 Broadway
London	New York
WC1B 3DP	NY 10018
UK	USA

www.bloomsbury.com

Bloomsbury is a registered trade mark of Bloomsbury Publishing Plc

First published as this collection 2014

Richard III, an Arab Tragedy, The Speaker's Progress © Sulayman Al Bassam 2014

The Al-Hamlet Summit © Sulayman Al Bassam 2006, 2014
Published by arrangement with University of Hertfordshire Press
All rights reserved

Introduction by Professor Graham Holderness © Bloomsbury Methuen Drama 2014

Sulayman Al Bassam has asserted his right under the Copyright, Designs and Patents
Act, 1988, to be identified as the author of this work.

British Library Cataloguing-in-Publication Data
A catalogue record for this book is available from the British Library.

ISBN: PB: 978-1-4725-2648-9
ePDF: 978-1-4725-3152-0
ePub: 978-1-4725-3332-6

Library of Congress Cataloging-in-Publication Data
A catalog record for this book is available from the Library of Congress.

Printed in India

Sulayman Al Bassam was born in Kuwait in 1972. He founded Zaoum Theatre in London in 1996, and SABAB Theatre, the company's Arabic arm, in 2002 with dramaturge and partner, Georgina Van Welie. Widely recognized as one of the leading and most outspoken contemporary Arab theatre makers, he produces work in English, French and Arabic and is regularly hosted at leading international venues across the world. Previous plays published in English include *Kalila wa Dimna – The Mirror for Princes* (Oberon Books, 2006).

Graham Holderness was born in Leeds and educated at state schools before attending Jesus College, Oxford. He has taught at the Open University, and at the universities of Oxford, Swansea, Roehampton and Hertfordshire. He is qualified to higher doctoral level in English and Drama, to doctoral level in Literature and Theology, and has published extensively in early modern and modern literature, drama and theology. Most of his 40 published books focus on Shakespeare, with particular interests in Shakespeare's history plays, Shakespeare and the media, Shakespeare editing, Shakespeare and contemporary culture and trans-national Shakespeare. His publications include: *D.H. Lawrence: History, Ideology and Fiction* (1982); *Shakespeare's History* (1985); *The Shakespeare Myth* (1988); *Shakespeare Out of Court: Dramatizations of Court Society* (1990); *Shakespeare: The Histories* (2000); and the trilogy *Cultural Shakespeare: Essays in the Shakespeare Myth* (2001), *Visual Shakespeare: Essays in Film and Television* (2002) and *Textual Shakespeare: Writing and the Word* (2003). His work on Arab Shakespeare has been published in journals such as *The European Journal of English Studies*, *Shakespeare Yearbook* and *Critical Survey*. Graham Holderness is also a novelist, poet and dramatist. His novel *The Prince of Denmark* was published in 2001; his poetry collection *Craeft* received a Poetry Book Society award in 2002; and his play *Wholly Writ*, about Shakespeare and the King James Bible, was recently performed at Shakespeare's Globe, and by Royal Shakespeare Company actors in Stratford-upon-Avon. He has also published research in literature and theology in journals such as *Harvard Theological Review*, *Journal for the Study of the*

New Testament, *Literature and Theology* and *Renaissance and Reformation*. Recent publications include *Shakespeare in Venice* (2009), *Nine Lives of William Shakespeare* (Bloomsbury/Arden Shakespeare, 2011), *Tales from Shakespeare: Creative Collisions* (Cambridge University Press, 2014) and *Re-writing Jesus: Christ in 20th Century Fiction and Film* (Bloomsbury, 2014). He is an elected Fellow of the English Association, the Royal Society of Arts, and the Royal Society of Medicine. Graham is Professor of English at the University of Hertfordshire, and Sub-deacon at the Parish Church of St Michael and All Angels, Bedford Park.

Contents

Introduction viii

Timeline of Conflict in the Middle East xvi

Author's Introduction xviii

The Al-Hamlet Summit 1

An Essay on Richard III, an Arab Tragedy; On the Burden of Text, Nation and Histories 59

Richard III, an Arab Tragedy 73

The Speaker's Progress 135

Introduction

Graham Holderness

1

The Arab Shakespeare Trilogy is a uniquely innovative dramatic experiment accomplished by Anglo-Kuwaiti dramatist Sulayman Al Bassam. It consists of three adaptations, written and produced between 2002 and 2011, which transplant Shakespeare plays into the geography, culture and language of the Middle East. Here presented in English-language versions, these plays have been, and continue to be, performed in Arabic and English, to audiences around the globe.

The three plays were not originally conceived as a trilogy, but rather grew organically into a complex totality, as the dramatist's engagement with Shakespeare deepened and expanded. *The Al-Hamlet Summit* was built on several earlier adaptations of *Hamlet*, and *An Arab Tragedy* written in response to a commission by the Royal Shakespeare Company. Nonetheless the three plays belong together, forming a uniquely comprehensive theatrical experiment. The three plays demonstrate an evolving response to the seismic political shifts that have disrupted the Middle East across this period, bringing both new freedoms and reinforced repression. And they comment upon one another, as well as their sources and their contemporary world. The plays adapted – *Hamlet*, *Richard III* and *Twelfth Night* – are drawn from three of the major Shakespearean genres: tragedy, history and comedy. Each adaptation makes use of its source in different ways, mixing genres in a very Shakespearean way. There is a savage comedy in the satire of *The Al-Hamlet Summit*, *An Arab Tragedy* plays out history partly as tragic farce, and *The Speaker's Progress* strikes a delicate balance between tragic containment and comic resistance.

These adaptations will appeal both to those interested in Shakespeare, and to those concerned with political and cultural events in the Arab world. They work upon the Shakespeare texts to produce new and unforeseen meanings; and they fashion dramatic forms that reflect in innovative ways on contemporary world events. They can be read and performed in English to illuminate such events for English speakers; and they can be seen performed in Arabic for Arabic speakers eager to find in Shakespeare some enlightening reflection on their own diverse societies.

2

Sulayman Al Bassam is one of the world's leading Arab dramatists. Born in Kuwait, son of a Kuwaiti father and a British mother, he was educated in Britain. He speaks Arabic, and writes in English; his works are translated from English into Arabic by others, with his own participation. Al Bassam's theatrical works, however, have been performed right around the world, particularly in America and Europe, as well as across the Middle East and North Africa. He is essentially a global playwright.

He has created original works drawing wholly on Arabic culture and tradition, such as his play *Kalila wa Dimna – The Mirror for Princes*, a radical adaptation of allegorical animal fables which explored the mechanics of Empire and the narratives of power, and was performed, in Arabic, in Tokyo, and at London's Barbican Centre in 2005. The play strongly argued the case for cultural and religious tolerance in the modern Arab and Western worlds. Most of Al Bassam's theatrical critique of his contemporary world has, however, been effected through his adaptations of Shakespeare, which now together form *The Arab Shakespeare Trilogy*.

3

The Al-Hamlet Summit was first performed in English in August 2002, as part of the Edinburgh International Fringe Festival, and in the same year won Best Performance and Best Director Awards at the 14th Cairo International Festival of Experimental

Theatre. Subsequently, as a result of a Japanese commission, the play moved into the Arabic language and undertook a world tour, playing in London, Singapore, Denmark, Seoul, Tokyo, Warsaw and Tehran. In his earlier experiments with *Hamlet*, Al Bassam had focused on adapting Shakespeare's text. *The Al-Hamlet Summit* by contrast jettisoned Shakespeare's language, and rewrote *Hamlet* into a modern English which attempted a concrete and objective translation of Arabic concepts and rhetoric into English, producing what the author called a 'cross-cultural construction'. The characters occupied a space akin to a political assembly, sitting at, and moving around, desks and chairs. In this new staging all of the characters were visible all of the time. Projection screens displayed the larger context of an empire desecrated by war.

Al Bassam's play maps a Middle Eastern political tragedy onto the template of Shakespeare's *Hamlet*. The key characters carry Shakespearean names, and occupy parallel situations within their own modern Middle Eastern world. Hamlet's father, the old ruler, has been poisoned, and his position usurped by Claudius his brother, who bore more than a passing resemblance to Saddam Hussein. Gertrude and Ophelia, Polonius and Laertes all play roles comparable to those of their Shakespearean namesakes, but redomesticated into an Islamic Arab context.

The regime is threatened, as Denmark is threatened at the beginning of *Hamlet*, by Fortinbras's troops lining the borders, and internally by the 'People's Liberation Brigade', which has been distributing leaflets claiming Old Hamlet was assassinated. Where Claudius in Shakespeare's play resolves the Norwegian threat by diplomacy, Claudius in *Al-Hamlet* responds with violence and atrocity. Fortinbras's army is backed by the West, 'armed with millions of dollars of foreign equipment'. Behind the suggestions of foreign intervention lies the West's greed for Arab oil (Claudius is obsessively concerned to protect the pipelines from sabotage). The West appears in the play in the shadowy persona of the Arms Dealer, who spoke English in the Arabic version, and was played by a woman in the English version. The Arms Dealer converses with, and supplied arms to, Hamlet, Ophelia, Claudius, Gertrude and, finally, Fortinbras. S/he will provide weapons to anyone prepared to pay, even if s/he is arming opponents.

In a scene which is the equivalent of *Hamlet* 3.3, instead of displaying remorse and praying for forgiveness, Claudius voices what is virtually a religion of oil and dollars.

> Oh God: Petro dollars. Teach me the meaning of petro
> dollars. I have no other God than you, I am created in your
> image, I seek guidance from you the All Seeing, the All
> Knowing Master of Worlds, Prosperity and Order ...

At the end of the play Fortinbras clearly intends to sustain this policy and this faith: 'It won't be easy, terrorism is not yet defeated, but the pipeline will be completed within a year.' In response to this context of corrupt and repressive power-politics, characters such as Hamlet and Ophelia find strategies of resistance and subversion that belong to the contemporary context, rather than to Shakespeare's play. Hamlet becomes a jihadist, and Ophelia a suicide-bomber. Shakespeare's rotten Denmark becomes a corrupt Middle Eastern regime, and Shakespeare's tragedy of revenge a war of terror against terror.

4

Al Bassam's next Shakespearean adaptation, his version of *Richard III*, was premiered at the Royal Shakespeare Theatre in Stratford as part of the RSC's 'Complete Works' project in 2007. The repertory consisted of 'mainstream' productions and parallel or alternative versions ('responses'). *An Arab Tragedy* was billed as a 'response' to Michael Boyd's production of *Richard III*, and was initially titled *Baghdad Richard*. The play was performed in Arabic (the first play in Arabic to be produced by the RSC), with the English text projected onto screens as surtitles, and with some scenes spoken in English. It was subsequently performed in Washington DC, Abu Dhabi, New York, Kuwait, Damascus, Paris and Amsterdam.

Although the play was set in an unnamed 'Gulf state', Al Bassam clearly did not want the play's frame of reference restricted, as some reviewers suggested it was, to the Gulf monarchies. Hence he broadened the scope of the piece to include the whole Middle East:

> More generally, the modern Middle East, like so many of Shakespeare's tragedies, offers a painful plethora of examples of how not to rule. Modern imperialism, tyranny, barbarism, oppression, plots, assassinations and civil wars are sadly becoming the rule not the exception in our region. The players in this grim game of politics, natural resources and strategic power are many, and like all the characters in *Richard III*, none are innocent; all have bloodied their hands.

Shakespeare's play is ripe for such analogies, replete as it is with arrests and executions, secret assassinations, political in-fighting and photo-opportunities, hostage-taking, character assassination and show trials, religious hypocrisy, forced confessions, usurpation, invasion and civil war. All these aspects of the plot were here 'Arabized' and transferred to the play's 'unnamed oil-rich kingdom or emirate'. The staging accentuated these parallels further. As in *The Al-Hamlet Summit*, back-projected images fleshed out the contingent context of despotism, military action, clandestine surveillance. Al Bassam's Buckingham is a double agent, secretly liaising with the Americans as he ostensibly supports Richard's bid for the throne. The screens recorded his coded email communications. Richmond was portrayed as a platitude-spouting Christian US general who at the play's conclusion announces the installation of an interim government. At the final point of the drama, just before the theatre collapses its illusions and decants us back out into our own world, we are here transported from 1400 to 2003, from Bosworth Field to Afghanistan or Iraq in the embattled Middle East of the twenty-first century.

5

Al Bassam's most recent production premiered in New York in 2011. *The Speaker's Progress* used *Twelfth Night* as a starting point to explore events in the Middle East. The play transformed Shakespeare's comedy into a satire on the political inertia of the Arab world, and a theatrical metaphor for the mechanisms of dissent. The production was strongly coloured by the 'Arab Spring', the succession of revolts against established regimes that have begun to rise up across the Arab world. Al Bassam comments:

> A new history is finding its voice among the millions across the Arab world who stood up and continue to stand – and fall – for dignity and freedom after decades of shame and oppression. This play, forged at the cusp of these two eras, has the fortune – and the responsibility – to be one of its platforms.

In an unnamed Arab country theatres have been shut down and theatrical performance criminalized. From a lectern, a former theatre producer, played by Al Bassam himself, explains to the audience that what he is presenting is not a play, but a reconstruction of a 1960s production based on the story of Shakespeare's *Twelfth Night*. The costumes and set resemble a scientific rather than an artistic context, with the actors wearing laboratory coats. Men and women remain at a distance from one another. An ominous camera sits in front of the stage, suggesting universal government surveillance.

The 1960s production of *Twelfth Night*, we understand, had the radical spirit of its time, especially in its irreverence towards moral and political authority. We see parts of it in black-and-white film on a large screen onstage, and hear Shakespearean dialogue adapted to a radical contemporary agenda: 'Music is the food of love and love is the blood of freedom and freedom is the mother of progress … How can you transform a country if you don't put women at its centre?' The government-sponsored revival played out on stage tries to empty the performance of any radical sexual or political content. But the actors run into trouble, simply by having a woman dress as a man. Shakespearean drama becomes a metaphor for radical dissent.

The reconstruction is performed by eight actors who are also 'not actors', the Speaker emphasizes, but 'envoys' from the Tourist Board and the Council of Virtue. Initially the actors obediently deliver the official programme. Gradually they begin to deviate from the script, and wander into politically dangerous territory. They burst into song; women change into dresses and take off their headscarves; they cry 'Freedom!'. People are arrested; voices are silenced; disobedience repressed. But the energy and humour of the Shakespearean drama continually explodes through the barriers of oppression. *The Speaker's Progress* is Sulayman Al Bassam's Arab Spring.

Bibliography

Aita, Sean, '*Twelfth Night*, or Inshallah', *Shakespeare Seminar*, Ausgabe 10, *Believing in Shakespeare: Faith and Doubt on the Elizabethan Stage*, Christina Wald and Felix Sprang (eds) (Weimar: Deutsche Shakespeare-Gesellschaft, 2012), pp. 39–52.

Al Bassam, Sulayman, 'Shakespeare, Global Debris and International Political Theatre', in *Doomed by Hope: Essays on Arab Theatre*, Eyad Houssami and Elias Khoury (eds) (London: Pluto Press, 2012).

Al-Khallili, Raja Khaleel, 'Political Villainy on the Modern Stage: Arabic Translations and Adaptations of Shakespeare's *Richard III*', *Canadian Social Science* 8:2 (2012), pp. 45–9.

Holderness, Graham, 'Arabesque: Shakespeare and Globalisation' (with Bryan Loughrey), *Essays and Studies*, 59, *Globalisation and its Discontents: Writing the Global Culture,* Stan Smith (ed.) (Leicester: English Association and Woodbridge: D. S. Brewer, 2006), pp. 24–46.

—'Introduction' to Sulayman Al Bassam, *The Al-Hamlet Summit* (Hatfield: University of Hertfordshire Press, 2006), pp. 9–19.

—'Arab Shakespeare: Sulayman Al Bassam's *The Al-Hamlet Summit*', *Culture, Language and Representation* 4, *Intercultural Communication* (July 2007), pp. 141–50.

—'From Summit to Tragedy: Sulayman Al Bassam's *Richard III* and Political Theatre', *Critical Survey* 19:3 (December 2007), pp. 106–25.

—'"Rudely Interrupted": Shakespeare and Terrorism' (with Bryan Loughrey), *Critical Survey* 19:3 (December 2007), pp. 126–42.

—'Shakespeare entre l'Orient et l'Occident', in Sulayman Al Bassam, *Richard III: une tragedie arabe* (Paris: L'avant-scene Theatre, 2008), pp. 66–8.

—'"Silence bleeds": Shakespeare across Borders – The Shakespearean Adaptations of Sulayman Al Bassam', *European Journal of English Studies* 12:1, *New Englishes* (Spring 2008), pp. 59–77.

Litvin, Margaret, 'Explosive Signifiers: Sulayman Al Bassam's Post-9/11 Odyssey', in *Shakespeare After 9/11* (special issue of *Shakespeare Yearbook*). Matthew Biberman, Julia Reinhard Lupton and Graham Holderness (eds) (Lewiston: Edwin Mellen Press, 2010), pp. 103–36.

—*Hamlet's Arab Journey: Shakespeare's Prince and Nasser's Ghost* (Princeton: Princeton University Press, 2011).

Timeline of Conflict in the Middle East

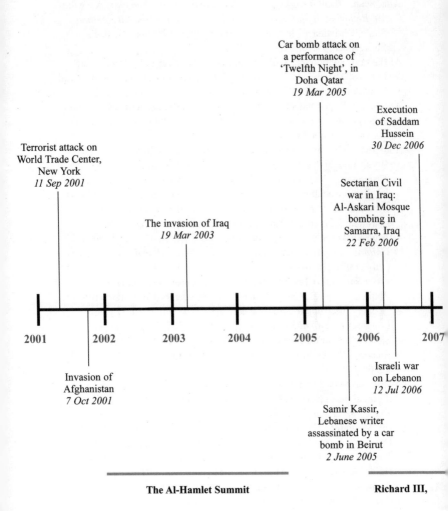

Car bomb attack on
a performance of
'Twelfth Night', in
Doha Qatar
19 Mar 2005

Execution
of Saddam
Hussein
30 Dec 2006

Terrorist attack on
World Trade Center,
New York
11 Sep 2001

Sectarian Civil
war in Iraq:
Al-Askari Mosque
bombing in
Samarra, Iraq
22 Feb 2006

The invasion of Iraq
19 Mar 2003

2001   2002   2003   2004   2005   2006   2007

Invasion of
Afghanistan
7 Oct 2001

Israeli war
on Lebanon
12 Jul 2006

Samir Kassir,
Lebanese writer
assassinated by a car
bomb in Beirut
2 June 2005

The Al-Hamlet Summit

Richard III,

The touring life of each production in the Trilogy.

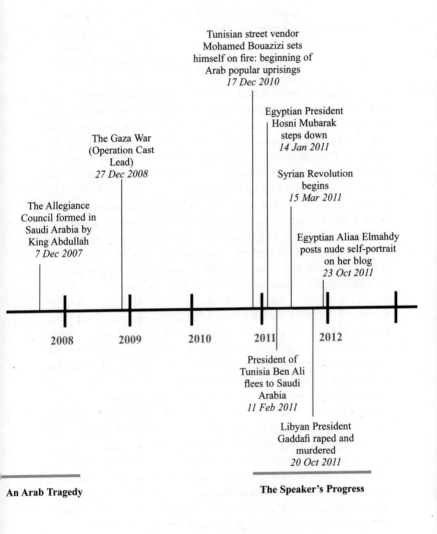

Tunisian street vendor
Mohamed Bouazizi sets
himself on fire: beginning of
Arab popular uprisings
17 Dec 2010

Egyptian President
Hosni Mubarak
steps down
14 Jan 2011

The Gaza War
(Operation Cast
Lead)
27 Dec 2008

Syrian Revolution
begins
15 Mar 2011

The Allegiance
Council formed in
Saudi Arabia by
King Abdullah
7 Dec 2007

Egyptian Aliaa Elmahdy
posts nude self-portrait
on her blog
23 Oct 2011

2008   2009   2010   2011   2012

President of
Tunisia Ben Ali
flees to Saudi
Arabia
11 Feb 2011

Libyan President
Gaddafi raped and
murdered
20 Oct 2011

An Arab Tragedy   **The Speaker's Progress**

Author's Introduction

The great storm howls above – the people groan.
The storm that annihilates the land roars below – the people
groan.
Lament for the City of Ur

This Trilogy was created over a decade between 11 September 2001 and the birth of the popular Arab uprisings, known as the Arab Spring, which began in January 2011. The plays are informed and inflected by concerns, issues and events pertaining to my perception of the Arab world during that first decade of the twenty-first century. They also address the charged, airless and perverse relationship between the Middle East and the West.

The tension between what the Shakespearean play tells and what I felt needed to be told is the defining principle that runs through these plays. The three plays are built, in varying degrees, out of Shakespearean caskets. They draw heavily on the structure, characterization and tenor of their Shakespearean inspiration and are explorations of themes found in *Hamlet*, *Richard III* and *Twelfth Night*. Extremism, corruption, power, kingship, identity, authoritarianism and sexuality are but a handful of the themes that attracted me to these texts, themes that gave promise of their potential as vehicles for politically charged, contemporary theatre pieces. But the conditions of creation and the radical violence of the world around me at the time of writing dictated a second, more urgent and highly contemporary prerogative onto these plays. It was this prerogative of urgency and relevance that led the texts to betray the Shakespearean text and explicitly flow into the particular moment of history – and geography – in which they were made. In this way, the plays carry the markings of the War on Terror, the Axis of Evil, Al Qaeda, Al-Jazeera, the birth of unfettered sectarian violence, invasions of foreign armies, oil at 130 dollars a barrel, military dictatorships, petro-fattened decadence, the collapse of old orders and the blasting effect of post-modernity on pre-modern societal structures.

The peculiar conditions of production that led to the creation and distribution of these works accentuated this tension. The plays were written and developed inside the Arab world for performance at international venues in other continents. *The Al-Hamlet Summit*, first presented in English at the Edinburgh Festival, was remade between Kuwait and Damascus for performance at the Tokyo International Festival; *Richard III* was commissioned by the Royal Shakespeare Company in the UK and made between Kuwait and Beirut; *The Speaker's Progress* was made in Damascus, Kuwait and Beirut and received its world premiere at the Brooklyn Academy of Music in New York.[1] Here was war: there was peace. Here were rampant poverty and obscurantism: there were mild social tensions and universal literacy rates. And, as if by chance, here comes Democracy proudly rolling in on the back of a tank! The radical disconnect between what was happening inside the Arab world – see timeline above – and the relative stability and tranquillity of the cities where the works were scheduled to receive their premieres became a mirror, in my mind, of the disconnect between the Shakespearean tale and the tale that needed to be told.

The overriding question, therefore, was never whether the original texts needed to be adapted or not, rather *how* to make the Shakespearean text carry a distinct agenda, another authorial voice without marring the first and diluting the second. How to render *Hamlet* a story about the birth of Islamic religious fanaticism fuelled by domestic corruption and Western opportunism? How to make *Richard III* into a cautionary tale about a crisis of succession in a petro-dollar monarchy? How to make *Twelfth Night* into the story of secularism and tolerance in the Arab world being devoured by religious censorship and state authoritarianism? More generally, how to make these concerns legible and engaging to international audiences unfamiliar with contextual detail of the Arab world, whilst simultaneously maintaining the relevance and provocation I wanted to deliver to Arab audiences. In both *The Al-Hamlet Summit* and *The Speaker's Progress*, I developed new texts and guided the storytelling through this new channel. With *Richard III*, I needed a different approach; more adaptive than transformative, reliant more

---

[1] The pieces, in their entirety, can be viewed online as part of the Massachusetts Institute of Technology's World Shakespeare Archive.

on transposition than composition; the process of this approach is explored in the essay that accompanies the play in this volume.

The Al-Hamlet Summit and *The Speaker's Progress* were originally written in English for performance in Arabic. I was schooled in Arabic until the age of 11 and, as a result, read and speak fluently but have never felt comfortable writing creatively in Arabic. Given these circumstances, I needed to find an effective way of translating the texts into Arabic. What began as an apparently simple task led me into a labyrinth of linguistic possibilities.

Translating drama from one language to another is, in any circumstance, a delicate task. Diplomats speaking at the UN perform in formatted, clear, tidy, transparent language in order to avoid any unwanted misunderstandings with other delegates. Metaphor, simile, assonance, dissonance, rhythm, wordplay and other tools of rhetoric and poetry are all unwelcome guests in international forums. But in drama, thankfully, it's the opposite: words are valued for their opacity, their violence, and their capacity to mesmerize, captivate, shock and be ambiguous. Consider translating, for instance, the English idiomatic greeting, 'Alright?'. In the absence of a defined context one might proffer a neutral equivalent of 'How are you?'. But if we define the context further and put this greeting into the mouth of, for example, an illegal immigrant worker herded in to meet the Head of the National Immigration Service in a state where illegal immigrants are shot on apprehension, when this worker says 'Alright?' then 'How are you?' no longer works in translation. It lacks the brazen provocation and casualness of 'Alright?'. It lacks the forward energy and inappropriateness of 'Aright?'. One would need to translate the equivalent of 'Yo dude!' or 'Wassup, man!' to get closer to the meaning. Both these vernacular greetings, in turn, bring with them intimations of age (young) and geographical location (North America) that would need to be consistently levelled with the character and location of the events in the story. When a play is written from beginning to end in one language and then translated into another, a balance of tone and meaning becomes achievable in the translated play. But when the play continues to be written *through* the process of translation, the writing process enters into a kind of ping-pong dynamic where ideas in one language ignite new ideas in the other. New meanings, new possibilities are created and new voices become heard through the migration into another language.

When I first started translating the pieces, I sought the help of venerable, certified translators. Every page that came back to me was like being hit over the head with hollow, dead wood. 'It's important', I'd object, 'that the Arabic carries a stylistic vigour, a modernity, a studied variety of tonal register.' 'But', the baffled, translator would reply, 'it's as accurate as it can be in Standard Arabic!' Standard Modern Arabic (S.M.A.) is a literary form of Arabic used across the Arab world in writing and formal speech. It is also the chosen medium of most twentieth-century Arab dramatists. Established and promoted in the early twentieth century, S.M.A. erases the idiomatic and vernacular aspects of spoken Arabic and successfully ensures understandability across wide geographical areas by proposing a whitewashed, comprehensible, standardized alternative. Partly as a result of this standard speak, today's Arabic is what's called a diglossic language. Different forms and varieties of the same language are used depending on the social context: a supremely Shakespearean linguistic model. The Arabic dialogue in the scripts needed to step beyond the Esperantan straitjacket of linguistic uniformity and leap into the churning waters of the diglossic language.

This decision liberated the dramatic text on so many levels: suddenly an overwhelming plethora of possibilities opened. So it was that extracts of dialogue, scraps of monologue, outdated translations of Shakespeare glossed with pen and covered in rewrites would end up in diverse hands. I'd call on friends, associates, poets, religious authorities, lawyers to propose ways of saying things. Political slogans, jokes, dictums, sayings, pre-Islamic poetry, Quranic verses, words that stopped being said by women two generations ago, slang: all were bona fide conveyors of meaning. Later, at the rehearsal stage, actors would apply their performance instinct to layer, add detail, feeling and resonance to the texts. In this way, the Arabic performance texts became living palimpsests that accrued the input, graffiti and inflection of many scribes.

The resultant meanings in Arabic would often migrate back into the original English version of the text and I would re-engage with the ping-pong process of translation, feeding back into the

English version of the script ideas from the freshly altered Arabic script. Only over time and through the act of repeated performance would the shifting, morphing palimpsest settle and crystallize into a definitive, stable text in both languages.

These plays bear witness to and are the artefacts of the workings of a troupe.[2] A motley band of theatre makers and actors from diverse origins, generations, beliefs and tribes with no fixed address who came together consistently over many years – whenever circumstance and provisions allowed – with belief, conviction and courage to develop, enhance and perform these plays across the cities of the world that made us welcome. I'd like to thank the scholars Professors Margaret Litvin and Graham Holderness, whose interest and close attention to these works fed, over the years, into the ways in which the work developed. Finally, the continuity of vision, commitment and support that made this Trilogy possible was given by one person: the dramaturge of the Trilogy and my partner, Georgina Van Welie – it is to her that this collection is dedicated.

Sulayman Al Bassam, 2014

---

[2] SABAB Theatre, www.sabab.org

The Al-Hamlet Summit

Delegates
Claudius – *The Ruler*
Gertrude – *His wife*
Hamlet – *Her son*
Polonius – *The Minister*
Ophelia – *His daughter*
Laertes – *His son*

Outsiders
Fortinbras
Arms Dealer
UN Messenger

Act One, Al-Fajr[1]

A conference hall containing six conference desks.
Downstage centre, a roughly constructed grave.
Claudius *throws a flower on the grave and exits.*

Scene One

Gertrude   Why is your face so black, Hamlet?

Hamlet   It must be syphilis; been with one too many whores, mama.

Gertrude   Is this wit?

Hamlet   Fact! There are many more whores than in my father's
time.

Enter **Laertes** *and* **Ophelia**.

Gertrude   Hamlet!

Hamlet   You should take a stroll, those tall buildings, lit with
neon; brothels, brothels!

Laertes   Welcome back, Prince. My condolences; may Allah
increase your wages in heaven.

Hamlet   And yours in brothels, Laertes.

Laertes   My Lord?

Hamlet   No, no ... I hold you in the highest esteem, Laertes;
your father was a loyal, devoted, loving subject to mine, and I rely
most entirely on your devotion to our line.

Enter **Polonius**.

Polonius   His Dread and most Honourable Majesty, All Mighty
Leader of the Armed Forces, Commander of Air, Land and
Sea; President Elect of this Noble Assembly begs your gracious
attentions – session has begun.

Enter **Claudius**, *all stand as the National Anthem bellows across
the conference hall.*

Claudius   In the Name of Allah, The Bounteous, The Merciful. *(The sound of the conference bell indicates the beginning of the session: all sit.)* By my decree ten thousand palms have been planted and two public gardens opened in my brother's memory. *(All clap.)* The time for mourning is over. Today the dawn bursts forth fertility and – like the phoenix that comes shimmering up in flames from its cold bed of dust – my wife from my brother's ashen hand has leapt, her cheek all moist with tears and wet with the dew of renewal, to partner me in this crowning enterprise: the dawn has risen upon the people of our nation: the New Democracy begins today! *(Assembly claps.)* The nation claps: I clap for the nation. We ride on the crest of a great wave, born of the will of the people and the needs of History: I am not its leader: I am its lamb. *(Clapping.)* Hamlet, you do not clap? Hamlet?

Hamlet   It is the heat, my Lord, it brings the worms up out of the earth and just beneath the film of our perfumes-

Claudius   No one doubts the enormity of your grief, Hamlet -

Hamlet   I am dazed by the stench of rot!

Claudius   You are morbid, when the world celebrates around you, you grieve while others rejoice, this fetish-sadness sits like a stain on the New Democracy: what is past is past, what is dead is dead, what rots will rot.

Hamlet   I'll spare you my afflictions, my studies await me; my flight leaves tonight.

Claudius   The invisible forces of evil besiege us from all sides: enemy leaflets circulate like rats in our midst; Fortinbras's troops armed with millions of dollars of foreign equipment are lined upon our border, if the city were quiet enough you could hear them breath; you will not leave.

Hamlet *rises from his desk.*

Gertrude   Hamlet, I am your mother. The University has long been the source of regressive trends amongst us, already it has changed you: your father and I have deemed it council to keep you away from such throbbing beds of lunacy.

Hamlet   Closer to your throbbing beds of shame.

Gertrude   The country weeps with you, Hamlet, its wounds are open, and need your balming presence. Do not tar your father's memory with such eager departure. Do not force knives into your mother's bleeding heart. Stay with us Hamlet.

Polonius   I will count.

They vote.

Hamlet   When I got off the plane I smelt her; on the runway, in his welcoming embrace in the guards' salute I smelt her. On his hand and on his cheek – her scent – on his neck and on his back and on his balls her scent. Oh God, I can smell her now. Oh filth, filth, he enters her, he goes inside, he does, he goes inside her again and again … I'll stay! *(* **Hamlet** *votes.)* I'll stay!

Claudius   Glorious solidarity blesses our nation's first assembly. Let enemies beware of the Nation United, let Fortinbras skulk upon our borders, I declare three days national holiday in celebration of our New Democracy.

Polonius   Come, secretaries and ministers: the press, the people, the world awaits.

A bell announces the end of the session.

Exit all except **Hamlet** *and* **Ophelia**.

Scene Two

Hamlet, **Ophelia**. *Prayers in the distance from many sides.*

Hamlet   Why are you spying on me?

Ophelia   I'm looking at you.

Hamlet   And I … am looking at you.

Ophelia   I will go, then.

Hamlet   No, no – Ophelia?

Ophelia   I'm here.

Hamlet   Has it been so long?

Ophelia   Three summers … I got your voice notes, thank you.

Hamlet   My voice notes …

Ophelia   I know them all by heart; 'when the skies fall in and the seas are set ablaze …'

Hamlet   It was a different world then.

Ophelia   And me?

Hamlet   You're a woman now.

Ophelia   Won't you look at me?

Hamlet   Now?

Ophelia   Why not?

Hamlet   Not now – I will, I will. I long to look at you, to stare at you, to drink from the sight of you, but not now. I can't. Perhaps it's the heat, my blood is not used to this heat, my blood is not what it used to be – I do love you, in my heart of hearts and with my own body I love you. Go now … *(Writing.)* Through the interminable night that awaits us … With your own eyes.

Jets pass in the distance overhead.

Scene Three

Enter **Polonius, Claudius**.

Polonius   I've got 300 men working round the clock gathering up the leaflets.

Claudius   Forget the leaflets, burn the townships, all of them – I want them all burnt by dawn.

Enter **Gertrude**.

Gertrude What's the schedule for tomorrow?

Polonius Breakfast with the Russians first thing, press conference, then it's the opening of the new parliament. Madame will be with us?

Gertrude Yes.

Ophelia *returns to her desk. A bell announces the beginning of the session.*

Claudius *(At his desk.)* What remains for today, Polonius?

Polonius My son, my Lord, asks your permission to leave the city.

Claudius Why?

Laertes To join the ranks of the valiant defenders of our nation's sovereignty.

Claudius Good, a young man like him needs to see some action. Let him be stationed in the South, in front of Fortinbras and overseeing the militias.

Laertes I will do all in my power to be worthy of this honour.

Claudius I'll make him a general.

Polonius My Lord!

Claudius Nothing is too much for the son of Polonius.

Polonius I am forever yours.

Claudius I thank you all for your devotion. Time is neither with us nor against us, our enemies are vigilant, they scurry while we sleep. I bid you all good night.

A bell announces the end of the session. Exit **Hamlet***,* **Laertes***,* **Ophelia***.*

Gertrude I have a proposal. It concerns Ophelia.

Polonius What has she done?

Gertrude Laertes is leaving. She will be so alone.

Polonius   She has many pursuits; she is an excellent pianist, reads profusely, rides regularly, speaks French, German and Mandarin-

Claudius   She is very beautiful.

Gertrude   Hamlet, given that he's staying with us, will have far too much time on his hands: Ophelia is vulnerable.

Polonius   Do you suspect my daughter of anything?

Gertrude   I am a woman, Polonius, and I sense the seeds of scandal before they are blasted on to the wind. I am also a mother and a wife. My son has long been of an inclination towards your French-speaking, piano-riding, horse-tinkling daughter and now he is of an age. I propose their marriage. Claudius?

Claudius   What has this to do with the New Democracy?

Polonius   It would be one of its symbols.

Claudius   It would entertain the press?

Polonius   A sense of shared responsibility, my Lord, may help the Prince overcome this negativity towards the New Order.

Claudius   Marriage would geld him.

Polonius   Madame, our house is no stranger to royalty; honour and blood have tied us together over centuries; my daughter will be delighted.

They vote. Motion carried.

Gertrude   Excellent.

Polonius   Marvellous.

Claudius   The future is ever brightening. To the New Democracy!

Polonius and Gertrude   The New Democracy!

A bell announces the end of the session.

Exit **Gertrude**.

Claudius   The townships, Polonius.

Polonius   I'll give orders to start the burning immediately.

They exit.

Scene Four

Laertes, *clearing his desk. Enter* **Ophelia**.

Ophelia   To the mountains?

Laertes   Yes.

Ophelia   You'll die, Laertes, they'll send me a YouTube of you hanging from a tree.

Laertes   I cannot do diplomacy. We sit and talk like drunkards, waiting for others to solve our problems.

Ophelia   Wait just a few days, things will settle.

Laertes   Nothing will settle Fortinbras but a bullet in his head. Look at me: I'll miss you. Your eyes, Ophelia, your eyes … They are not the innocent jades they used to be, another colour has tinged them. A little sparkle, or, or, or a little breeze, or, or, or a little … aching? An aching in your eyes, Ophelia, the aching of virgin fields for the plough? When the world lies frightened in its bed do you pour lotions over your body and move in time with the breeze? I know you do, but that is not what courts and Kings are for, is it? What are they for? Capturing, invading, sacking, splitting: virgin thighs, virgin honour, virgin sex; your name, spiked on the royal cock, our titles spattered with royal cum, and poor sister of Laertes left heaped on the floor among the broken shells of promises and the burnt-out shitloads of gold. Never, Ophelia, never! Tame this lust in your eyes, tame it, woman, before I tame it for you.

Enter **Polonius**.

Polonius   General Laertes!

Laertes *salutes his father and exits.*

Ophelia   Don't leave me.

Polonius   They tell me you have been lurking in orchards with the Prince Hamlet as the sun goes down. Or was it by the pool? Where do you lurk exactly?

Ophelia   We walk sometimes at dusk before the evening prayers.

Polonius   Don't walk at dusk, don't walk at night, don't walk at dawn and don't walk at noon. Right now I want to be able to hear your footsteps at all times, wherever you walk will be within the orbit of my hearing, within the circle of my infinite love; right now my love describes the boundaries of your universe; don't walk outside it into the abyss beyond, where your footsteps and your cries will go unheard. What's the time?

Ophelia   Near midnight.

Polonius   Get to bed, there may be trouble tonight.

Polonius *returns to his desk.* **Gertrude** *enters* **Claudius***'s office, climbs onto his desk and raised her skirt.*

Scene Five

Hamlet*, praying at his father's grave.*

Hamlet   Let the skies fall in and the seas be set ablaze, let the material world collapse and markets go untended; let wild beasts roam through cities and infant girls be buried alive for no crime; make hell fires burn fiercely and bring paradise near; but lay the records upon, inspire me with your command, show me my labours, I hold my life in no esteem, I carry not an atom's weight of good, I have grown fat with idle life, let me not be mad, but lay the records upon, inspire me with your command, inspire me with your command – *(The love-making in the conference room climaxes.)* who's there? Who is it?

Arms Dealer   A friend.

Hamlet   What do you want?

Arms Dealer   No, please I understand you perfectly. Sorry, I'm–

Hamlet   I know who you are.

Arms Dealer   Not disturbing you am I? I–

Hamlet   Stay.

Arms Dealer   Needed some air: couldn't breathe in the hotel.

Hamlet   It's the fires, they've started the fires.

Arms Dealer   Mmm … Your father was a great man, the world is not the same for his loss.

Hamlet   Are you American?

Arms Dealer   *(Quoting.)* 'Vast oceans of savagery consume the world, false authority towers from Mecca to Jerusalem, from Jerusalem to the Americas and man is on the brink of a great precipice.'[2]

Hamlet   How do you know that? Those are his words.

Arms Dealer *hands him a green leaflet.*

Hamlet   I can't see, give me a light.

He holds out a lighter.

Hamlet   *(Reading.)* 'Forensic evidence leaked from the post mortem indicates that our great leader was murdered. His cardiac arrest was induced by sodium nitrate injected into his ear via a syringe, an assassination technique used by the secret police under the leadership of his brother and assassin Claudius.' Where did you find this?

Arms Dealer   They're all over.

Hamlet   *(Reading on.)* 'Whilst Hamlet, the late King's son, continues to lead the life of the murtad[3] dissolute, gambling and whoring the nation's millions in the playgrounds of Europe.' Oh God! 'The People's – the People's' – bring the light closer – 'Liberation Brigade will avenge this sickening murder and will show no mercy to those who weep and mourn, weep and gnash their teeth' *(The* **Arms Dealer** *sets fire to the leaflet.)* … the evil forces of imperialism have found a willing agent in the figure of Claudius!

Arms Dealer *withdraws.*

Screaming jets pass overhead; hundreds of leaflets fall from the sky.

Hamlet   'Raise your might and God's holy wrath against the horned Satan that soils our earth and the Greater Satan that enslaves our people and the world. We will not rest until God's labours are done. We will not rest until His labours are done.'

Hamlet *gathers an armful of leaflets and exits.*

Scene Six

Ophelia *at her desk,* **Hamlet** *enters.*

Hamlet   *(Shaking.)* My father's murdered.

Ophelia *holds him for a long time, he weeps.*

Ophelia   I'm here – I'm here –

Hamlet   Be with me –

Ophelia   Always.

Hamlet   Hold me.

Ophelia   I love you – I love you.

Black out.

Act Two, Al-Zuhr

Scene One

Morning.

Ophelia *alone at her desk, wearing a headscarf.*

Polonius *(At his desk.)* Today is a very good-looking day, correct? A day for positive images, rousing words, transparent communication and I need you to look the part, Ophelia … what the hell is that? Are you mad? *(Walks briskly over to her and snatches her headscarf.)* What's this?

Ophelia I'm more comfortable like this.

Polonius You look like a terrorist! Do you know how many photographers are out there? Why are you crying?

Ophelia Last night–

Polonius Last night what?

Ophelia Hamlet …

Polonius Hamlet!

Ophelia Needed some help with his speech, but the speech was not making sense; shells fell all night, the fires burnt all night and the electricity cut out around three. It was a bad night – that is all!

Hamlet *enters, goes to* **Claudius***'s desk, takes out files, scours through papers and written memos.*

Polonius *(Finding green PLF leaflets.)* Where did you get these?

Ophelia I don't know.

Polonius Answer me!

Ophelia He brought them.

Polonius This runs deep, Ophelia, very deep. I only hope I can save you from the fallout. Come with me. Come, come, come. *(Senses someone rummaging at* **Claudius***'s desk.)* Hamlet? *(***Hamlet** *runs away.)* Hamlet!

Scene Two

Enter **Arms Dealer**, **Claudius**.

Arms Dealer   Your Highness! Power suits you. You look like a King.

Claudius   I was not expecting you so soon.

Arms Dealer   Early bird catches the worm.

Claudius   And blood draws flies.

Arms Dealer   Buzz, buzz, Claude.

Claudius   Keep your voice down.

Arms Dealer   This is a most echoey corridor, you should have it filled: busts, statues, fallen enemies, stuffed and garroted, I know some excellent sculptors.

Claudius   How long will you be staying with us?

Arms Dealer   As long as I am welcome.

Claudius   We are preparing for war. It may not be in your interests to stay here very long.

Arms Dealer   I'm on a little tour. He called me yesterday, most upset I have not been to visit him yet, you know how emotional he gets – 'You filthy double-crosser, you promised me this, that – be careful, you're not dealing with the Chechnyans now!' – *(Laughs.)*

Claudius   Who's this?

Arms Dealer   Fortinbras!

Claudius   *Inshallah*, everything's okay?

Arms Dealer   He's so endearing, so forward-looking, so modern somehow.

Claudius   I'll send you the thing you like. I'm so happy you are with us.

Arms Dealer   So am I.

Claudius   We'll have a party.

Arms Dealer   No!

Claudius   Yes, a large one. I want you to meet the ministers.

Arms Dealer   I'd love to meet them, of course.

Claudius   Tomorrow – this evening! I'll arrange it. You must excuse me. The new parliament's opening in – *(Looks to his watch.)*

Arms Dealer   Two hours and 12 minutes – I know. Good luck.

Scene Three

Bell announces the beginning of the session.

Polonius   A minister's loyalty to his King and country goes beyond the rational bonds of duty. A love that defies the usual spheres of human employment. A love that, in my case, can be compared to the loyalty of the last soldier, that unsung hero, who, knee-deep in comrades' blood, surrounded by thousands of enemy tanks, helicopters, infantry and mortar, swells with the knowledge of imminent death, bulges with patriotism, fires the last rounds from his outdated Russian rifle and falls struck by a bullet to the heart that continues to beat for at least two hours more! Irrational love! Absolute devotion! Complete surrender to the will of King and country – THAT is what I offer.

Gertrude   Does my breakfast have to suffer this man's devotion?

Polonius   My breakfasts are yours, Madam.

Claudius   Explain yourself.

Polonius   *(Adjusts his position.)* If I were able to explain this matter *to* myself, I would be much better placed to explain myself; but this matter is far beyond ... Your son is mad, Madam! Mad! He is being drawn further and further into extremist circles of thought and action and he is mad, I tell you!

Claudius   The parliament opens in less than an hour.

Polonius   A matter of minutes: Ophelia.

Ophelia *stands up and reads* **Hamlet***'s poems.*

Ophelia   The refugee who stands at the wire fence of your heart –
no numbers to his name, no credit, no guns;
all sewage and exile,
lays siege to your soul, with the pain of his songs.

Polonius   Note the paranoiac tendency in this innocent-seeming foul-smelling ditty. Note the distrust of all authority.

Ophelia   When the worlds fall apart
And the skies cave in

(Enter **Hamlet***.)*

When hell fires consume the light
And paradise is brought nearer this earth:
On that day, know that I am looking for you.

(Exit **Hamlet***.)*

Polonius   Note the apocalyptic imagery. Note the yearning for violent and comprehensive change to the world order. I have studies that will elucidate further on the links between this sort of fantasy and terrorist activities.

Gertrude   These poems are the work of an adolescent, Polonius. They prove nothing!

Polonius   Now, look at what I found in his drawers! *(Displays PLF leaflets.)* Not one, not ten, but thousands of them, thousands!

Claudius   This is capital!

Ophelia   Grief can force–

Gertrude   Grief, yes! Grief!

Ophelia   Temporary insanity!

Claudius   The marriage must be delayed.

Ophelia   What marriage?

Gertrude   Until we have more proof of how far his grief may have changed him.

Claudius   More proof then, Polonius?

Ophelia   What marriage?

Polonius   My daughter will supply proof.

Ophelia   What marriage!!

Gertrude   Really? How?

Polonius   Ophelia?

Ophelia   Yes?

Polonius   The next time you meet with Hamlet you will ask him – in a roundabout and honeyed way – questions like, 'Where have you been? What have you been writing? What are you doing with your nights?'–

Ophelia   You think I can do that?

Gertrude   You'll make an excellent liar.

Ophelia   I lack your Highness's skill.

Gertrude   What did she say?

Claudius   We were all born bad liars, you'll learn. Ask him – 'Do you go to the mosques?'

Polonius   'Who are your friends? What are they called?'

Claudius   'What are you reading?'

Gertrude   Someone should be with her, she could lie.

Polonius   We'll be with her, Madam, leave it to me: *(Proposing a motion.)* 'The Royal Marriage to be delayed, pending further proof of the Prince's seditious leanings.'

They vote: the motion is carried. **Ophelia** *exits.*

Claudius   'They Deceive and God Deceives, but God is the greatest of Deceivers!'[4]

Bell announces the end of the session: all exit.

Scene Four

Hamlet *alone near the grave. In the distance we hear the sound of a military band and pronouncements on the occasion of the opening of the New Parliament.*

Hamlet   The villages of my heart have been emptied,
their pavements orphaned to the wind.
all spirit of man in me aged between 14 and 60
has been taken down to the waterfront
and settled head-first in the shallows.

When noon walks across the square like a widow,
I am the ghost bell that swings on churches
I am the minaret with its tongue in the sand
I am the child with a bullet in its arm weeping amongst the rocks;
I am the mute that contemplates the ape
while the wind writes my shame upon the sea.

Enter **Arms Dealer**.

Arms Dealer   You're not at the opening.

Hamlet   Celebration's lost its charms.

Arms Dealer   We're alike, we prefer being in the shadows.

Hamlet   Are you following me?

Arms Dealer   Maybe.

Hamlet   How's the hotel?

Arms Dealer   Been upgraded. There's a lot of talk about you: some people think you're still in Europe, others say you're planning to escape, but nobody really knows what you're doing, do they?

Hamlet   *(Looking at the horizon.)* When I was young the horizon had more colours, more light, more promise …

Polonius: Your son is mad, Madam! Mad!
Monadhil Daood and Nicholas Daniel. Photo by Arne Magnussen.

Arms Dealer   I was thinking, perhaps, we could be friends. You need someone to confide in and I know what it is like to be isolated. You have a great future, we would like to develop something with you, promote your agenda.

Hamlet   What do you know about phosphorus?

Arms Dealer   It makes little white puffs of smoke, like a barbecue.

Hamlet   Does it burn?

Arms Dealer   Haven't you heard the story of the gravedigger's baby?

Hamlet   Tell me.

Arms Dealer   When the curfew was over, the baby was five days dead, and they brought it the gravedigger. He prepared a deep and narrow grave, and when the prayers were done, he shovelled the first mound of earth into it: the tiny corpse exploded into flames and the gravedigger was blinded. That's phosphorus.

Hamlet   Can you sell me some?

Arms Dealer   I can.

Hamlet   Good.

Arms Dealer   It is necessary for a prince to understand how to avail himself of the beast and the man. If men were entirely good this would not hold, but because–

An explosion in the distance, the military band has gone silent and is replaced by sirens.

Hamlet   What was that?

Arms Dealer   I've no idea.

They exit together, hurriedly.

Scene Five

Enter **Claudius**, **Polonius**.

Claudius   Find them!

Polonius   No one has claimed responsibility, no tip-offs, no calls, nothing.

Claudius   The pipeline is on the rocks–

Polonius   I have got 20 PLF members under torture–

Claudius   The investors are terrified!

Polonius   The Shia leaders are being rounded up, I've got 50 mobile squadrons in a net around the city, men scouring the sewers, whoever they are, they will not escape me.

Claudius   I want the car-bombers' faces across the papers by tomorrow. Or I'll write your resignation for you.

Enter **Laertes**.

Polonius   I have summoned you Laertes to brief us on developments in the South.

Claudius   What news with you, Laertes?

Laertes   My lord, the signs of war are gathering fast. Until this morning, Fortinbras had three thousand men stationed 20 miles south of our border. Apart from two small skirmishes, all has been quiet for the last two days. But one hour before dawn a convoy appeared on the horizon that threw fear into the souls of our men and had civilian families running in droves for their cars. Over the hills came not a convoy, but a juggernaut, a 12-mile column of Merkava and British Centurion tanks – three tanks abreast – moving at pace towards our border. It was as if Fortinbras's entire army was advancing as one giant armoured centipede. The Merkavas and the Centurions tore up the tarmac surface of the highway as they advanced and bathed the landscape in a blue fog of exhaust smoke. They have moved up so much equipment that the coastal highway and the sea are covered with tanks and heavy artillery for 20 miles.[5]

Claudius   We are familiar with these tactics, Laertes, I see no cause for alarm.

Hamlet *enters carrying a piece of an exploded car. He affects deafness.*

Polonius   Where were you?

Hamlet   Sorry I'm late. Have you seen the traffic?

Laertes   *(To* **Claudius***.)* No cause for alarm, my Lord?

Polonius   You weren't at the parliament.

Hamlet   What?

Polonius   Parliament!

Claudius   *(To* **Laertes***.)* None.

Hamlet   Lament? Lament!?

Polonius   Where were you?

Hamlet   I'm finished with laments. Tell Uncle. Finished. There's a party out there! Hundreds, thousands, all spattered in blood, screaming in the streets! Ecstatic masses foaming with nationalistic ecstasy. It's brilliant!

Claudius   Hamlet, there was a terrorist attack at the opening.

Hamlet   Here we are. Look, oh look!

Claudius   A terrorist attack.

Hamlet   Quack? What Quack? Quack quack! I found this!

Polonius   He's mad!

Hamlet   It's a trophy. I'm giving it to Ophelia as a sign of my bleeding heart! No, too sad. I'm giving it to Uncle! Yes! Uncle! Give me a kiss and I'll give you this trophy.

Claudius   We'll leave him.

Hamlet   Oh come, Uncle, your kisses aren't as prized as Ophelia's lips. Please take it, Uncle, give it to mother as a sign of your mis-shaped love, oh, yes she'll take it. Uncle, the nation's will is in my arms, take it from me–

Polonius   My lord, we're leaving you now.

Hamlet   Uncle! Uncle!

Black out.

Act Three, Al-Asr

Scene One A

Time: 7:45 AM.

Arms Dealer   Parliament opened with a bang!

Polonius   Listen to this. *(Opens a folder and reads.)* 'The treacherous enemy are dwarves. They spit at the giant, but the giant picks them up and crushes them. They are traitors, pirates and mercenaries.'

Arms Dealer   We call them terrorists.

Polonius   I like this word. Will you write it for me? *(Offering him a pen.)*

Arms Dealer   Of course. *(Writing.)*

Polonius   Terro-ri!

Arms Dealer   Terro-rist.

Polonius   Terror-roo!

Arms Dealer   Terror-rist.

Polonius   Terror – um!

Arms Dealer   Terrorist!

Polonius   Terrorist! Excellent word, much money in this word.

Arms Dealer   Yes … About the money.

Polonius   Money? No problem, no problem.

Arms Dealer   When?

Polonius   When? When. What does it mean, 'when'?

Arms Dealer   Upon signing of the contract.

Polonius   In full?

Arms Dealer   *(***Arms Dealer** *seizes* **Polonius***'s skull and kisses him.)* In full! *(Exits.)*

Polonius   My pen … Terrorist!

Scene One B

Time: 10:15 AM.

Hamlet   Who is Claudius?

Laertes   You don't get it, do you?

Hamlet   Who is he?

Laertes   Our supreme and sovereign leader.

Hamlet   Take my eyes, my nose, my sword, my women! Are you a tribesman, Laertes?

Laertes   What do you want? The labourer has no factory to work in and the thinkers are all asthmatic and wheezing.

Hamlet   'As you are, in such a way you will be ruled.'[6]

Laertes   The people need a God!

Hamlet   Fine. I know where you stand.

Laertes   Forcing internal division is political suicide: the strategy of an angry child.

Hamlet   He is a murderer.

Laertes   So are all leaders.

Hamlet   He killed my father.

Laertes   Fortinbras wrote that line, it's enemy propaganda and you know it.

Hamlet   I'll prove it!

Laertes   Well, let me know.

Hamlet   I want you with me here, Laertes, the real fight is here.

Laertes   And let me know when you've finished.

Hamlet   What?

Laertes   … apologizing for your own futility.

Scene One C

Time: 13:30 PM.

Gertrude   Where was that – Paris?

Arms Dealer   Zurich.

Gertrude   Of course! Zurich! And how are your dogs?

Arms Dealer   I've just acquired a magnificent Pekinese stud.

Gertrude   And I have my Mexican Hairless bitch – we must introduce them!

Arms Dealer   What a monster we will make.

Gertrude   You are such a charmer.

Arms Dealer   You are such a purebred!

Gertrude   Is there anything I can do for you?

Arms Dealer   You are so kind. Anything I can do for you?

Gertrude   You're so cavalier! I don't want to trouble you, but I have a farm in the South – my private retreat: it needs some work, it doesn't feel safe any more and I was wondering if you might–

Arms Dealer   I just love the countryside! I believe I'm already familiar with the place.

Gertrude   Really?

Arms Dealer   *(Showing her photos.)* This it? You look so magnificent in your natural state!

Gertrude   I'll keep these if you don't mind.

Arms Dealer   Only copies, I'm afraid.

Gertrude   As I said, it needs tighter security.

Arms Dealer   My pleasure. Where are we going?

Gertrude   To the sea, you don't mind do you?

Arms Dealer   I smell it from here.

Scene One D

Time: 13:32 PM.

Hamlet   The enemy on the border is the illusion they feed you, the illusion they want you to believe.

Laertes   People are dying every day, I see them, I see the bombs that kill them, I see the soldiers that fire them, I hear the politicians that direct them, it's not an illusion.

Hamlet   The real enemy is here, in the palace, amongst us.

Laertes   There will be no nation to fight over unless we defeat Fortinbras.

Hamlet   We'll have no nation to lose unless we destroy the rot that devours it from within.

Laertes   Hamlet, May God be with you. I'm leaving you this. *(Places a pistol on the table.)*

Exit **Laertes**.

Hamlet   Laertes! My brother.

Scene Two

Gertrude *is presenting jewellery to* **Ophelia**: *a necklace, a bracelet, a ring.*[7]

Ophelia   Who are these from?

Gertrude   From Hamlet! Now listen to me; no politics, no religion. Talk about love, not sex, love. He's so *sensitive*, he cannot bear *vulgarity* – ask him about his poems, ask for some

more, nothing silly or girlish, please. You know how intelligent he
is, you must keep him interested!

Ophelia   A–

Gertrude   And don't cry! When you are married, you'll look
back at all this and laugh out loud.

Ophelia   We will, we'll laugh.

Hamlet   *(At his desk, holding the pistol* **Laertes** *left him.)*
It doesn't weigh much, why should it?
It delivers. It has a number on it. It's well made;
its coil, mechanism, bolt and trigger have
evolved over centuries, its secrets embezzled
from father to son, it is a perfect machine.
It is mine to polish with Egyptian cottons
while I career dreamsick, from office to office,
slowly murdering the fire that made my soul,
feeding my disease from door to door,
round and round this porn shop of sores.
No martyr's passion blazing in this body,
no vision of heaven,
no yearning for justice, no aching for change,
my intestine is like a pig's:
it baulks at nothing;
my hatred as imperfect as my love;
nothing heroic, nothing repulsive,
just a futile mediocrity, made bearable by my disease,
that drowns with a torturer's patience and criminal ease
the fires that made my soul
from here to the day I die.
(Reading the serial number on the pistol.) 552497.
The disease I carry is stronger than me,
This disease I call Myself.
The self is a bitch that won't let go.

Enter **Claudius** *and* **Polonius***, disguised as women, wearing long
black abbayas and burkas.*

Claudius   Thank you, Gertrude.

Gertrude *corrects the black abayya that covers* **Claudius**. *She exits.*

Polonius *and* **Claudius** *prompt* **Ophelia** *in the opening lines of this dialogue.*

Ophelia   Hamlet, I am praying for you.

Claudius *taps her on the back to speak louder.*

Ophelia   Hamlet, I am praying for you.

Hamlet   Ophelia! I can hear your prayers.

Ophelia   Thank you for your gifts.

Hamlet   What gifts?

Ophelia   It doesn't matter.

Hamlet   I don't know if I have ever told you …

Ophelia   Don't …

Hamlet   I must, I have this terrible need to change myself, or rather, rather there is a change that is coming …

Ophelia   Don't tell me now–

Hamlet   … and if I don't tell you now–

Ophelia   Tell me now, then, tell me, speak!

Hamlet   Ophelia?

Ophelia   Yes.

Hamlet   What gifts? What gifts! *(Long pause.)* Has it come?

Ophelia   What?

Hamlet   The hour that takes you away from me?

Ophelia   No!

Hamlet   Must I be forced to hate you now?

Ophelia   No! It is far away, very far.

Hamlet   But the hour has come.

Ophelia   I am still here.

Hamlet   No, no you are gone.

Ophelia   You love me.

Hamlet   No, no: I do not blame you, but, but, but …

Ophelia   Try to love me …

Hamlet   Nor can I forgive you, you do understand?

Ophelia   Don't do this.

Hamlet   How can I love you?

Ophelia   Try …

Claudius *and* **Polonius** *smother her mouth.*

Hamlet   I will clean this land, I will make it pure, I understand, I do understand, but I will cleanse it for you, I will prepare it for your return, even if it costs me my life, I will clean it, I will purge it, blood will flow, I will make blood flow in torrents, I swear in my father's name, I swear in the name of Allah but you will return, Ophelia, you will return. *(Exits.)*

Ophelia   *(Sung.)*
My master, where are you going?
Ai! Why don't you take me with you?
Take me to the town.
Ai! To sell me to the *bazargi*
For a pinch of gold
To gild the palace door.[8]

Exit **Ophelia**. *A bell announces the beginning of the session.*

Gertrude   She is ruining my son's mind. I want her sent to the farms.

Polonius   What farms, Madam?

Gertrude   The work farms in the south. She can work on mine. She is to go.

Polonius   Madam is enraged. This ugliness offends her and blurs her judgement–

Claudius   Gertrude, we refuse haste.

Gertrude   I insist.

Claudius   Polonius, let her seek refuge outside the city for a few days. Marriage will not be spoken of again. It puts our son in ill-humour. Investments are however crucial to the economy at this stage of the war-effort, there are car bombs exploding at every corner, we have not seen a tourist in weeks and his temperament seems regressive and unconducive to the common good; national security demands that Hamlet too is sent away. Where to, Madam?

Gertrude   Beirut?

Polonius   Too many militias.

Gertrude   Damascus?

Claudius   Too many lions.

Polonius   Cairo?

Gertrude   Too many loafers. Sana'a?

Polonius   Too many rebels.

Claudius   Rabat?

Gertrude   Too many druggies.

Claudius   Khartoum?

Polonius   Too many blacks.

Gertrude   Jeddah?

Claudius   Too many sticks.

Gertrude   Tehran?

Claudius   Too many turbans.

Polonius   Paris?

Claudius   Too many women.

Gertrude   Washington?

Polonius   He'd never get in.

Claudius   London?

Polonius and Gertrude   London!![9]

Claudius   Get him on the next plane to London, call the foreign secretary, tell him he's coming to gamble along Piccadilly, book him three months at The Berkeley and give him a state credit card.

Polonius   My Lord, Fortinbras's tanks shelled the airport this morning, the tarmac is in ribbons.

Claudius   Close the highway, he can use that to take off.

Polonius   I'll count.

They vote.

Polonius   Carried.

Gertrude   My son cannot leave without a proper send-off!

Polonius   She's right, it might reflect badly.

Claudius   A party, then!

Polonius   A small state occasion.

Jets pass overhead.

A bomb blast in the distance.

Claudius   The future is bright. I thank you.

A bell indicates the end of the session.

Delegates rise to leave. **Claudius** *lingers momentarily in the corridor.*

Enter **Hamlet**.

Hamlet   Hell's plagues on your mother and your mother's mother and your mother's mother's mother. Do not gawp at me you imperialist lackey! Don't stare you leader-by-proxy! Agent! Do you know whose son I am! His name makes you tremble!!

Claudius *exits.*

Hamlet   Futile man! *(To the musicians.)* Hey you. Play for me, would you? Play an old, old *maqām.*

They play.

Scene Three

Ophelia   Are you the devil?

Arms Dealer   Are you attracted to me, young lady?

Ophelia   If I am?

Arms Dealer   Have you ever been with a man before? Alone in the dark?

Ophelia   *(Silence.)*

Arms Dealer   You are trembling, come closer.

Ophelia   Lean your face towards me, close your eyes.

She pulls out a knife.

Arms Dealer   You're so passionate*! (He twists her arm and throws her to the floor.)* Oh, the sweet yelp of pain – angels of the night, hide your virgin faces; the devil has his cock up one of your flock! What do you want, Ophelia, tell me I'll satisfy you, what is it you want?

Ophelia   I want a bomb. Qumbila!

Arms Dealer   Qubla? A kiss?

Ophelia   Qumbila – a bomb.

Arms Dealer   A kiss! Say it again!

Ophelia   Qumbila!

Arms Dealer   Qumbila!

Ophelia   A bomb.

Arms Dealer   Kiss!

Ophelia   Bomb!

Arms Dealer   Bomb!

Ophelia   Kiss!

Arms Dealer   A little one or a big one?

Ophelia   Any.

Scene Four

Hamlet *standing on the edge of the central area of playing space, an area thus far unused in performance.*[10]

Hamlet   This empty space. Why is it empty? This pit our words fall into peat-like and mulch, where secrets fester and moult into dross, dirty little space no one dares cross. Here … *(He enters the empty space.)* in this dark, oily lake of lies, I see swans; here I'll dig and dance and jig, loop earthworms into a tie and set light the royal tips and vaginal lips that top their living and tail our dead. There'll be screaming in corridors and bodies lurching between the lawn sprinklers in naked, animal haste. Who then could say Hamlet stood by and did nothing?

Scene Five

Polonius, *reading a map, enters the empty space, followed by* **Gertrude**.

Gertrude   Here?

Polonius   Yes.

Gertrude   Are you sure, Polonius?

Polonius   He was most insistent, Madame, he even drew me a map!

Gertrude   Let me see.

Claudius *enters.*

Claudius   You're joking!

Gertrude   Claudius, it's his last night.

Claudius   Find somewhere else.

Gertrude   Don't be ridiculous!

Claudius   I have never stood there, no one has ever stood there, I do not see why I should stand there to humour the whims of your sick child.

Gertrude   Claudius, please!

Claudius   Polonius, get out of there immediately!

Enter **Arms Dealer***, bursting into the empty space.*

Arms Dealer   Good evening, your majesties.

Gertrude   Hello! What a surprise.

Claudius *enters the empty space.*

Claudius   We have been waiting for you.

Arms Dealer   Hamlet told me you were having a little occasion.

Claudius   I am so happy you could make it.

Arms Dealer   You look splendid, Madame.

Gertrude   *Merci. (Enter* **Ophelia***.)* God, Ophelia, you look half dead.

Polonius   She has been a little under the weather.

Ophelia   I have been throwing up all afternoon.

Arms Dealer   Poor child, do you have a fever?

Ophelia   Don't touch me!

Gertrude   She is upset that Hamlet is leaving.

Polonius   On the contrary, she is upset because she is leaving tomorrow.

Arms Dealer   I'm only trying to help.

Polonius   Thank you!

Claudius   Television been arranged?

Polonius   They're filming as we speak. Delayed transmission of course.

Claudius   What's the order of events?

Polonius   We'll shake hands and embrace, swig some juice and before you know it he'll be on the plane.

Claudius   I'm sweating.

Polonius   I'm sorry. *(***Polonius*** dabs ***Claudius****'s brow with a handkerchief.)*

Enter **Hamlet** *with a hobby horse, dressed as an Abbasid general. This scene is performed by* **Hamlet** *with hysterical speed.*

Hamlet   Good evening, tribe, family, friends.

Gertrude   Hamlet! What is this nonsense?

Hamlet   Nonsense! I am preparing for war, haven't you heard the enemy are on the borders! Ask him! Tonight we honour the elders! And stroke the horse! The horse of war!

Polonius   *(Humouring him.)* Why is your horse blinkered, my Lord?

Hamlet   To protect it from the glances of envy and Ophelia's poisoned smile.

Arms Dealer   Is the horse hungry, my Lord?

Hamlet   Ravenous, always! Horse of war!

Arms Dealer   A horse of war must munch, my Lord! *(***Arms Dealer*** offers a handful of sugar cubes.)*

Hamlet   Ah! Sugar cubes, what a noble warrior! Please feed the horse of war. Uncle, as with all things, you must start. Ummm …

Hamlet *lunges at* **Claudius** *and stabs him with a stage knife.* **Claudius** *gasps.* **Hamlet** *withdraws the stage knife, pushes the blade in with his finger and laughs. His horse's head droops.*

Oh, it's dying! Sodium Nitrate, Uncle quickly! Oh, if mother could weep, my horse might rise again. Not one little tear, mother? Dried up? *(Gertrude approaches Hamlet, who gnaws her ear viciously.)* Oh, look, it's rising, thank God mother has some moistness left in her! Risen erect. Uncle could not kill it! Of course not, indigestion, that's all – *(Hamlet grabs Polonius by the testicles.)* Horse of WAR! Munch some more! Stroke it, mother, but don't kiss it, it is a very randy horse. Ophelia – you look pregnant – Uncle have you sent her to the front yet? *(The horse nuzzles Ophelia's breast and rubs its head against her groin.)* She really must make a visit – raise the morale of all those thousands! *(Ophelia exits. Hamlet to the Arms Dealer.)* Oh, but you, you are all sugar, it's enough for the horse to lick your hand. Now let us sing: 'Our blood is the price – oh cowards you are lice – but Glory gory Glory to the Nation!' *(The assembled join in reluctantly.)* To war! I thank you all. To war! To war!

Exit **Hamlet**.

Claudius   We are sending him to London, for tests.

Arms Dealer   I know some specialists.

Gertrude   Really? Perhaps you could give me their names.

Arms Dealer   Gladly.

Polonius   How would you like to present this affair to the nation, my Lord?

Claudius   As is!

Gertrude   What is that terrible noise?

Claudius   What's going on, Polonius?

Polonius   Some interference on the intercom, don't worry, my Lord.

Hamlet, *over the conference loudspeakers.*

Hamlet   Wait, please, wait, please.

Claudius   Sort this out!

Arms Dealer   Perhaps he's armed.

Claudius   Polonius, you dog!

Hamlet   There's more, my dears.

Claudius   This is unacceptable.

Over the speakers, **Hamlet***'s voice repeating 'Uncle, Uncle'.*

Gertrude   Hamlet, stop this immediately.

Claudius   Polonius – your gun!

Hamlet   Ladies and Gentlemen! I come in peace! *(Rounds of sniper gunfire, offstage.)*

Polonius   Guards! Guards! Guards!

Scene Six

A bell announces the beginning of the session.

Claudius   He is a threat! I want him liquidated.

Gertrude   I'll speak to him.

Claudius   Polonius!

Polonius   My Lord!

Gertrude   I said I'll speak to him.

Claudius   Give the order.

Gertrude   *(Forcefully.)* My sex, Claudius! My sex tames your allies, my sex undermines your enemies, galvanizes the masses and underwrites your loans. Nothing without me, do you realize? Nothing! I will speak to my son.

Claudius   By tomorrow.

Polonius   I'll accompany Madam. We must fear the worst.

Claudius   Thank you, my wife. *(Exit* **Gertrude***.)* I've emptied the funds, Polonius, you'll see me later about your needs.

Polonius   The generals are waiting for your directi–

Claudius   Let them wait!

Exit **Polonius**.

Scene Seven

Claudius   *(Alone, opening a briefcase full of dollars.)* Oh God:
Petro dollars. Teach me the meaning of petro dollars.

I have no other God than you, I am created in your image, I
seek guidance from you the All Seeing, the All Knowing Master
of Worlds, Prosperity and Order. This *(Extracting a bundle of
dollars.)* for the nation's new satellite TV station, this *(Another
bundle of dollars.)* for God's satellite; this for the epic about my
valiant life, this for God's film industry; this for surveillance
networks across the capital, this for God's installation people; this
for primary, secondary and higher; this for God's curricula; this
for me. This for the leader of the opposition party; this for the
Austrian torturer; this for the editor of the national press – or is
he dead? This for the MD of Crude Futures: all of Heaven's gifts
down to the cracks of their arses and I, the poor, sluttish Arab,
forgoing billions to worship you: I am transparent, so transparent
my flesh emerges like calf's milk – I beg you, Lord, give me the
recognition I need and help me calculate what is good.

Is it not charm, is it not consummate charm to slouch on silk
cushions and fuck and be fucked by all the flesh dollars can buy? I
am a fine apprentice, do I not learn well what you taught me? This
for you, oh God.

Help me, Lord, help me – your angelic ministers defame me,
they portray me as a murderer, a trafficker of toxins, a strangler
of children, why is this God? I lie naked before you while they
deafen you with abuse. Let me not be disagreeable to you, God,
I do not compete with you, how could these packets of human
flesh compete with your infinity? I am your agent, nor am I an ill
partner for your gluttony and endless filth.

I do not try to be pure: I have learnt so much filth, I eat filth, I
am an artist of filth, I make mounds of human bodies, sacrifices to
your glory, I adore the stench of rotting peasants gassed with your

technology, I am a descendant of the Prophet, Peace be Upon Him, and you, you are God. Your angelic ministers want to eliminate me, throw me like Lucifer from the lap of your mercy, but who brought me here oh God let us not forget, who put me here?

In front of your beneficence, I am a naked mortal, full of awe: my ugliness is not unbearable, *surely* it is not? My nose is not so hooked is it, my eyes so diabolical as when you offered me your Washington virgins and CIA opium. *Oh, God, my ugliness does not offend you now, does it?*

Your plutonium, your loans, your democratic filth that drips off your ecstatic crowds – I want them all, Oh God; I want your Vaseline smiles and I want your pimp-ridden plutocracies; I want your world shafting bank; I want it shafting me now – offer me the shafting hand of redemption – *oh God let us be dirty together, won't you?*

Without you, I cannot bear to be myself, cannot, cannot bear it.

Enter **Hamlet** *holding a pistol to* **Claudius**'s *head.*

Hamlet   The only way to change the geography of a conflict is to have infantry on the ground firing bullets into flesh. I am the infantryman, this is the basement that reeks of human faeces and rotting meat, my emotion is the emotion of the fighter who wants to stop an invasion; here my enemy cowers, human, alone. I see the drops of sweat glistening on your skin, I can smell your fear, I can hear you breathing, I feel your fear now: stop breathing … Stop … breathing: stop breathing!

Hamlet's *conviction collapses. He returns to his desk.*

Black out.

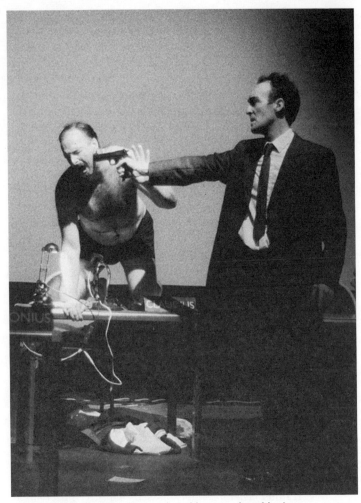

Hamlet: Stop … breathing: stop breathing!
Nigel Barrett and Neil Edmond. Photo by Stephanie Kulbach.

Act Four, Al-Maghrib

Scene One

Enter **Polonius**.

Polonius   *(Seeing* **Claudius**, *semi-naked.)* My Lord!

Claudius   Tell the generals: we are alone.

Exit **Claudius**.

Enter **Gertrude**. **Polonius** *hunkers at his desk, unseen by* **Hamlet**.

A bell announces the beginning of the session.

Gertrude   Hamlet, you are a threat to state security.

Hamlet   Mother, you are a threat to state morality.

Gertrude   Is it drugs?

Hamlet   Is it sex?

Gertrude   Talk to me, child, are you collaborating with the mullahs?

Hamlet   No! It is I who ask you: do you commune with the devil, Madam? Is he by you now, enveloping you? Ha! Does the devil sit by you Gertrude, does he whisper in your ear? Ha! Does he hold you to him and thrust his hand onto your breast – is he there? Ha! Is he there? Is he there?

Gertrude   *(To* **Polonius**.*)* Leave now.

Polonius *prepares to leave the desk in haste, clattering objects as he moves.* **Hamlet** *hears the clattering and shoots the pistol in the direction of* **Claudius**'*s desk, killing* **Polonius**.

Gertrude   What is this!

Hamlet   From Allah we emerge and to Allah we return. Run, blood, run across the sewers and the graves, stop up the mouths of vermin and hypocrites, the squall that begins in the East moves with mighty power over the seas. Oh, mother, mother, I am still so young, so young to feel this weight of heaven. Your husband is a murderer!

Gertrude   You are the murderer!

Hamlet   He murdered my father!

Gertrude   Your father died of his own failures!

Hamlet   You are with the devil! The power of the djinn has eaten your mind.

Gertrude   Look at you, panting! Do you desire me? You are sick!

Hamlet   The earth spins faster in its rapture as the dawn of truth approaches. *(He strikes her.)*

Gertrude   You dare to hit me!

Hamlet   I dare more!

Gertrude   Bastard son of a bastard father!

Hamlet   God cannot forget your iniquities!

Gertrude   *(She spits on him.)* On you and on your father.

Hamlet   You have outwhored Babylon!

Gertrude   Get off me, get your hands off me.

Hamlet   God's sharia allows you to be married to your husband's brother only when there are no other men available to you. Will you not learn, woman?

Gertrude   I will have you stripped in the streets for this, I will open your stomach with a breadknife.

Hamlet   Rude Gertrude!

Gertrude   I will hang your balls from my balcony!

Hamlet   In the time of the Prophet it happened thus, a whore passed from King to pauper, from murderer to thief, until she found the path. Will you learn? Lewd Gertrude! In the tractions of your loins do you not think on death, woman? Has lust made you mad?

Covers her eyes and raises his weapon to her womb.

Remember Allah!
Remember Allah!
Remember Allah!

Over the loudpeaker: Verse 28, Surra 5 of the Holy Qur'an: 'And never say to your father or mother tut, nor hold their names in vain.' **Hamlet**, *hearing this Qur'anic voice, is cowed and amazed. He returns sheepishly to his desk.*

Gertrude   Gertrude will never forget this shame you have poured upon her, this stain of blood will not fade.

Gertrude *exits.*

Hamlet   Oh God, I have trespassed! Beware a mother's vengeance.

Mother forgive me.
Mother?
Mother?
Mother?
Mother?

Scene Two

Enter **Claudius**.

Claudius   Terrorist, terrorist, terrorist! Hamlet, we will not let an insidious terrorist coward push our nation to the brink of collapse–³

Hamlet   Look around you: embargoes closing in from all sides, world leaders refuse your calls, my country's assets are frozen.

Claudius   Your terror will not dictate our policy – you are exiled!

Hamlet   So it has come to this?

Claudius   Yes. Now. Go.

Hamlet: It is a far, far better thing I do now than I have ever done. Where is it to, Uncle?

Claudius   London!

Hamlet   Ah! London! I will not be alone. I will eat little, grow thin, write tracts and become the prized animal of European liberals. Good, Uncle, good; a perfect choice. Farewell Uncle!

Claudius   I would dismember you now were it not for the glare of the world upon us. Let their lights die down – then I'll strike, invisible.

Scene Three

Claudius   Do you think I am a monkey?

Arms Dealer   Not at all, Claudius.

Claudius   Take this. *(Handing a list.)*

Arms Dealer   *(Reads.)* Five hundred howitzers, 12 B-2s, 4 Stealths, 5 submarines, 500 Centurions; 17 Cruise Missiles; 200 hawks; 300 sparrows; one million rounds of ammunition … a week?

Claudius   Don't ever tell anybody I am a monkey, or I'll have you shot, do you understand?

Arms Dealer   Perfectly.

Claudius   Shhh.

Arms Dealer   Shhh.

Scene Four

Enter **Hamlet***, barefoot.*

Hamlet   Peace be upon the grave dwellers.
I am ill, grave dwellers, I am ill,
sick with the lies of the living,
that have spread like shredded pieces of the night,
its end resembling its beginning.

How is the end, grave dwellers, how is it worse than the beginning?
I will pass these 40 nights amongst you,
your bones will be my books, your skulls will be my lights,
I will hold my tongue amongst you,
And eat from the dreams of the dead.

He enters his father's grave.

Scene Five

Gertrude   Claudius! I'm drunk!

Claudius   *(On a phone.)* I want the guard doubled on the
ammunition dump – forget the water supply …

Gertrude   How can you leave me here, I'm drunk!

Claudius   What about the reserve generators? I know that …
hold them back as long as you can … I will reward you, General.

Enter **Laertes**.

Laertes   The dogs of war are baying for your blood; Claudius,
give me my father!

Claudius   I have missed you, Laertes.

Laertes   Where is my father?

Claudius   Missed your ethical guidance–

Gertrude   It's a coup!

Claudius   Your loyal instinct, your strength. I can feel the
sniper's aim warming the back of my head – what has happened to
you, Laertes?

Gertrude   Little Laertes is mounting a coup!

Laertes   I am waiting for your answer.

Gertrude   Tell me Laertes, if you kill him, will you marry me?

Laertes   I'll brand you like a devil's trollop.

Gertrude   I'm not your mother, I'm your Queen!

Laertes   Give me my father!

Claudius   Your father is with me. He has lost his voice. He asks me to ask you why you have betrayed him.

Laertes   I never betrayed him.

Claudius   He asks you if he ever left you wanting for anything.

Gertrude   Raise your voice, Polonius!

Laertes   Why should I want for anything?

Claudius   Then why do you align your militias with Fortinbras? Is it for shekels, is it arms, is it fear? What do you lack, Laertes?

Laertes   Show me my father.

Claudius   Hamlet holds him hostage.

Laertes   Where?

Gertrude   In his grave.

Claudius   Gertrude!

Gertrude   Dead!

Ophelia *appears, veiled, in a pre-recorded video message on the conference projection screen.*

Ophelia   Are you recording? Can I start? In the Name of God The Bounteous, The Merciful.

Laertes   Ophelia!

Claudius   She is mad, Laertes.

Ophelia   The one who has turned me into a refugee has made a bomb of me.[11]

I have tried to speak the language of women,
I have tried to forgive, on many nights I severed my tongue
but my silence bleeds from my mouth.
Here I am the animal that the world forgets,
I have try to speak the language of man

but lying no good no change can make to it
of injustice in life.
I want people outside to know this
that I will express with with my body what is not
able for to express politics and mighty nations
so I go to my God pure in my soul in my dignity I am pure.

Scene Six

Claudius *and* **Laertes** *removing the body of* **Polonius**.

Claudius   Hamlet kills Laertes' father, Hamlet drives Laertes' sister out of her mind. Have Laertes' guns fallen silent?

Laertes   What are you asking me?

Claudius   Should I smother the press, should we keep this quiet?

Laertes   Announce it! And I will announce my revenge in the plumes of smoke that raze his villages to the ground.

Claudius   Those villages are your villages, I am making you Lord of the Southern region, we'll announce it tonight. *(A bomb blast, followed by a woman's scream.)* Will you let me guide you?

Laertes   I'm listening.

Claudius   Hamlet is returning with a flock of émigrés, communists and degenerate scum that the nation spat out years ago. He claims to be the Redeemer! To raise support among the people, he'll go the Holy Mosque to lead the Friday prayers; you will meet him there with one thousand men dressed in the nation's colours. Half accidentally, your men will trample on the holy grounds and cause such brazen offence to his zealots that they will revolt there and then with stones, with tyres, with–

Laertes   What for?!

Claudius   A third of the nation.

Laertes   A third for me and a third for my father.

Claudius   Half!

Laertes   I'll do it. And if you lie, I'll kill you.

Enter **Gertrude** *with a scream.*

Gertrude   Your sister, Laertes. She came into the palace when the sun fell into the trees. When the guards were warm and droopy like the oranges her eyes were blazing and alive, her dress swollen with the wind as if with a phantom child, with fantastic wailing she moved beyond the guards into the courtyard, a swollen angel against the black sweep of the tarmac; I went towards her and as she raised her arms as if to salute the world, a button came loose from her shirt and tittered onto the steps, I remember this button, Laertes, this little disc of mother of pearl; and leaning over to retrieve it on my way home when – no – when I was there, then in the rolling flesh in the twitching limbs and her body was a well I washed myself in: how hot it felt across my face, how hot her lungs, her intestines how hot.

No one is exempt.
Exemption is impossible.
I carry my guilt, I carry it.
But, but, but …
Am I still beautiful?

Black out.

Act Five, Al-Isha'a

Scene One

At **Ophelia**'*s desk, delegates laying flowers, muttering prayers.*

Hamlet *enters in a short white thowb, with a long beard – he has transformed his appearance into that of a radical Islamist leader.*

Hamlet   I loved her with a noble love and I killed him. I killed your father and mine. Yes, you can look at me now, Mother. I did this out of love. What is the death of the father, Laertes, what is it, when defeat is the very secret of our rebirth?

Gertrude   Hamlet!

Hamlet   Mourn your father's death to salute the living, but do not mourn to salute the King! I want you with me in the reshaping of our nation.

Laertes   You bastard!

Hamlet   Is this fidelity, Laertes? Standing next to the King in your father's very shoes – you are not the shadow of the dead, you are death's double!

Laertes *strikes him.*

So be it! What now? Do we saddle our horses, sharpen our swords, make prayers and prepare for Kufa,[12] thus do we rise again! Can that be? Can it be?

The other delegates return swiftly to their desks. The **Arms Dealer** *is, for the first time, inside the Conference space.*

Arms Dealer   Your father would be proud.

Hamlet   He's dead and you – still here?

Arms Dealer   I'm leaving. My work's done. I am happy to have been of assistance.

Hamlet   I will make you regret your assistance.

Arms Dealer   Destiny makes dark plans–

Hamlet   Get out.

Arms Dealer   However we curse and spit, kick and writhe–

Hamlet   Out!

Arms Dealer   We nudge each other towards its manifestation!

Hamlet   Out!

Arms Dealer   Fortinbras will be so pleased!

Hamlet   Depart!

Arms Dealer   Farewell.

Scene Two

Hamlet   He who can speak without tables, without chairs, without lies let them speak. *(Silence.)* This silence will bury us all.

A bell announces the beginning of the session.

I bear witness that there is no God but Allah and that Mohammad is his messenger. I Hamlet, son of Hamlet, son of Hamlet and the rightful heir to the throne of this nation. My rule will crush the fingers of thieving bureaucrats, neutralize the hypocrites, tame the fires of debauchery that engulf our cities and return our noble people to the path of God. Our enemies comprehend only the language of blood, for this, the time for the pen has passed and we enter the era of the sword.[13] Do not pretend amazement! Violence breeds princes and princes breed violence, that is our curse! And may God raise the souls of his Martyrs to the gardens of Heaven.

All vote. **Gertrude** *hesitates.*

Gertrude   Whereto this madness, Hamlet, whereto?

Hamlet   No more words please, mother, words are dead, they died on our tongues. Admonishment is a weak form of faith, now we must mouth meaning with our flesh.

Gertrude *votes. War has been declared. The conference bells begins to repeat.*

Enter a messenger.

Messenger   The world community represented in the UN has sent you this message: that it is prepared to send peace-keeping troops to the region and organize a summit meeting chaired by disinterested political figures to discuss the differences between your parties.

Hamlet   Invite your masters to a private showing to see the dead dancing before their killers,[14] perhaps you can teach us the art of slaughter and acquittal of the slaughterer.

Messenger   You will die, Hamlet.

Hamlet   No, I hurry to the dignity of life and the eternity of death.

Exit messenger.

Hamlet and the UN Messenger
Sulayman Al Bassam and Mariam Ali with Nicholas
Daniel in projection. Photo by Arne Magnussen.

Claudius   History lays its greatest challenge before us. Just two hours ago, our forces–

A pre-recording (sound or video) of **Claudius**'*s address to the nation begins to play and overtakes* **Claudius**'*s words in the event sphere on stage.*

Each delegate, realizing what has happened, rises from his/her desk, clears away the last objects of value to them, opens the munitions box beside them,[15] *takes out the weapon inside it and walks forward, listening blankly yet astutely to the speech being broadcast overhead.*

As they walk forward, press reports intercut into **Claudius**'*s speech, reporting the latest developments of the civil war. Amongst these gathering mounds of information, each delegate waits for the confirmation of their own deaths. When they hear it, they collapse, dead. To be performed in a manner as simple and unforced as possible.*

Claudius's address to the nation   Just two hours ago, our forces began an attack on terrorist positions belonging to Hamlet and his army. These continue as I speak.

   This conflict began when Hamlet laid siege to our democracy, our values and our people through a brutal series of kidnappings and terrorist bombings that have killed many innocent victims and shocked the world community. Tonight this battle has been joined.

The following news reports, intercut into **Claudius**'*s address, should be broadcast in Arabic:*

News Report   The streets of the capital are in flames, buildings have collapsed through the endless onslaught of air attacks from the F-16 fighter planes still loyal to the King. Meanwhile, Hamlet the Crown Prince, and leader of the People's Free Army–

Claudius's address to the nation   As I report to you, air attacks are under way against military targets within the city. We are determined to knock out his lethal, nuclear potential; destroy his chemical facilities; much of his artillery and tanks will be destroyed.

News Report   In an unconfirmed report, Queen Gertrude

has been killed whilst trying to prevent the King's tanks from surrounding her son, who is trapped inside The Grand Mosque.

Gertrude *dies.*

Claudius's *address to the nation*   We will crush the terror not with books and speeches, but with courage and good judgement and responsibility. Some may ask why act now? Why not wait? The answer is clear: the world can wait no longer.

News Report   As the Multinational Peace-keeping Force sent by the United Nations arrived off the coast yesterday, General Laertes and Hamlet's forces were engaged in arm-to-arm combat throughout the streets. At 10am this morning reports arrived that Laertes was struck by mortar fire and his condition is described as critical.

Laertes *dies.*

Claudius's *address to the nation*   I had hoped that when we took our decision in historic debate to exile him, that would be the end of this criminal life, but I have been proved wrong, and today the world will see that error corrected.

News Report   The Army are sparing no one. Hamlet is firing mortars from the Mosque and Claudius is firing from the palace.

Claudius *dies.*

Hamlet   In the name of God I have invented a curse
That writes the history of other nations in my own people's blood.

Perhaps the hardest thing is to find the courage to wake in the morning and face this landscape of ruins that are our lands.

This perception of truth too late,
Is hell.

Hamlet *dies. Pause.*

Enter **Fortinbras**.

Fortinbras   Faeces, intestines and sweat. Only dead humans can smell like that. I have biblical claims upon this land, it is empty and barren and my presence here is a fact that has not been invented. It won't be easy, terrorism is not yet defeated, but the pipeline will be completed within a year, and hunger will be eradicated, the homeless will find refuge, the old will die and the young will forget, the poor will find wealth and this barren land will be seen to bloom. What we see here can never happen to us. For this is the dawn and the birth of the Greater

Is–

White noise fills the conference room censoring **Fortinbras**'s *voice.* **Fortinbras** *repeats the attempt to pronounce the word and, each time, his voice is overwhelmed by white noise.*

Iz– …
Izzzz … Izzzzzzzz … aaaaaa.

Sudden silence.

With your help the future will be bright. Go, let the turrets point … West; let the centurions salute.

Arms Dealer *enters and walks towards* **Fortinbras** *incredibly slowly.*

Black out.

End

Notes

1 The names of each act are those of the five daily prayers in Islam.
   They are descriptions of mood, not indicators of time.
2 'Vast oceans of savagery consume the world', from the Introduction
   to Al-Sayid Qutb's, 'Milestones'.
3 'Murtad' Arabic, meaning 'apostate'.
4 'God is the greatest of Deceivers' Qur'an (3:54).
5 From Robert Fisk's 'Pity the Nation'.
6 '… as you are, so you will be ruled', from the Hadith of the Prophet
   Muhammad.
7 The collection of jewellery is the 'Taqam' that is traditionally
   presented by the groom's mother to Arab brides.
8 The words are a rough translation of a Bosnian folk song.
9 Other capital cities used in performance:
   • Baghdad?
     Too many Iranians!
   • Kuwait?
     Too many Saudis!
   • Dubai?
     Too many Russians!
   • Qatar?
     Where?
   • Bahrain?
     Too many tombs!
10 The empty space. See the technical drawing overleaf of the
   conference corridors shown in grey and the resultant empty space in
   the middle of the stage:

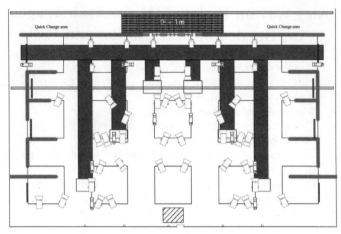

11   The opening line is from a poem by the Palestinian poet, Mahmoud
     Darwish.
12   The Battle of Kufa was the first in which Muslims fought against
     fellow Muslims.
13   Osama bin Laden in a speech broadcast by Al-Jazeera Satellite
     Television on 7 October 2001.
14   This image is from a poem by contemporary Iraqi poet, Muthafar
     Al-Nawab.
15   This stage direction is, perhaps, too directorial. In my own production
     of the piece, the munitions boxes referred to were brought into the
     conference room by each of the delegates after their meeting with the
     Arms Dealer. Laertes, who is the only delegate who does not meet
     with the Arms Dealer, picks up his father's munitions box. However,
     it is entirely possible to imagine this scene taking place with no
     munitions boxes, no movement downstage of the delegates and so on,
     in the same way that it is possible to imagine playing this entire text
     without conference desks, corridors and other paraphernalia of the
     conference or international summit

An Essay on Richard III, an Arab Tragedy; On the Burden of Text, Nation and Histories

> ***Judge:*** *Where do you live?*
> ***Saddam Hussein:*** *I live in every Iraqi's house.*

Summer, 2006. Kuwait. The writer/adaptor commissioned by the Royal Shakespeare Company, UK, to make a free adaptation of Richard III, under the working title of 'The Baghdad Richard', finds himself hosting many a circular conversation with himself. One of these conversations leads him to write to a friend – an Iraqi director and dramaturge who he'd admired greatly and who had recently died.[1]

31 July 2006

Dear Awni,

I miss you.

I'm in the process of working on the commission of 'Richard III' for the Royal Shakespeare Company that we spoke about last time we met. Tyranny – though we've dollops of it – is a thing I'm having difficulty finding a suitable dramatic language for. When I agreed to make this project, Saddam Hussein was still in hiding; his Tikriti hovel was not on the radar, Operation Red Dawn was still Operation Desert Scorpion or Planet X or whatever it was and, back then, it seemed fitting – or at least not completely outrageous – to call it: 'The Baghdad Richard'.

The title immediately struck a chord with the RSC – and the sensationalist British media – and now I feel like I'm nailed to a board, having to write a kind of 50s Schlock Horror B-movie that would inevitably only reconfirm all the hysterical prejudices against us that I want rid of!!

Richard III is above all a history play and you can't go overlaying one nation's history onto another without deforming one and oblite- rating the other. The only way *Richard III* can become *The Baghdad Richard* is if you approximate, colonize and completely truncate the contemporary history of Iraq – I'm not prepared to do it. Or, you treat *Richard III* as a portrait of the pathology of a tyrant – in which case it would be more interesting to look at *Macbeth* because at least *Macbeth* has domestic settings and the translations into Arabic are better! In any case, now that Saddam's going to be hung and Iraq is creeping towards civil war under the stewardship of its belligerently irresponsible Occupiers, it seems doubly inappropriate to revisit Saddam's rise and fall. To do that now would cast the glow of mythology onto the man and end up excusing the American Occupation in one way or another.

You were acutely aware of the terrible stranglehold placed on cross-cultural work by the prejudice of Arab Nationalism, on the one hand and Western reductionism, on the other. You knew what it felt like holding a handful of adders.

And the worst thing – a kind of Buddhist hell – our history wants to die, yet is perpetually reborn. Baghdad is already at one remove from Baghdad and Richard at two removes from Richard. Baghdad is Riyadh, Damascus, Tehran, Cairo, Tel Aviv and elsewhere. Richard is Saddam, Abdullah, Bashar, Dick Cheney and others. The disease is already metastatic and the origin needs to be found. But it's not hiding in the story of a provincial thug turned megalomaniac psychopath – his story is anecdotal; the region's history is not.

'Our armies do not come into your cities and lands as conquerors or enemies, but as liberators', also sprach Sir Stanley Maude … standing proud in Baghdad in 1917. Old Stanley might have made a sprightly – Etonian – Baghdad Richard, but he died of cholera too fast. Or was it dysentery? Why can't our history promptly die of cholera?

Not far north from here, car bombs are going off, limbs are flying into the air; death and revenge are becoming part of the natural order. In Lebanon, the Israelis are back to bombing the hell out of civilians to create new temples to their Gods of destruction. Perhaps that is a way forward: take from Shakespeare a strand of Gloucester's DNA, the helixes of revenge … a root to cure us with.

I remember you told me about a baker woman – was she in Mosul? – who baked her bread on her doorstep and resolutely continued to bake her bread on her doorstep when snipers and bullets filled the air above her head. That would be worth showing – wouldn't it?

Awni, I miss you terribly and just wanted to let you know.

Yours,
Sulayman

* * *

Gloucester: *Foul wrinkled witch, what makest thou in my*
sight?
Queen Margaret: *But repetition of what thou hast marr'd.*

Having been summoned to the Ministry of Information in his home country; told how lucky he was to be a citizen of his home country commissioned to present the first-ever play in Arabic in the birthplace of the Bard; told that Richard III required a lot of horses to be made properly and warned against upsetting anyone in the home country by imagining that a citizen of the home country could go naming the play after the capital city of the neighbouring country especially given that Richard was, after all, a proper English name, the writer/adaptor went home and wrote the following story. An Arab political allegory.

It was a dusty, death-mouth night in mid-July and the only thing that moved inside the perimeter of the palace were the man-eating carp in the artificial lake and the sprinklers over the lawns. It was on this night that the dream, delivered by an angel, came to the Leader.

Troubled by its portent, the Leader cancelled the next morning's meetings and prowled through his gardens distracted. Drinking glass upon glass of fresh almond juice, his Jordanian cook ordered 30 sacks of almonds; National Television aired the same football match ten times in a row as no other instructions were forthcoming and the day was remembered as one in which the children of the city were too fearful to lay traps for birds and muezzins at the top of their minarets struggled with vertigo.

That evening, in a faux Baroque chamber, the members of the Revolutionary Command Council were summoned to discuss the Leader's dream. Of the original 22 members of this Council, seven men remained. Fourteen eyes around an oval of Italian marble and the Leader at its head.

The Leader described his dream in detail and, in turn, each member of the Revolutionary Command Council was invited – by a flick of his finger – to comment on it. The

*dream had left a positive impression on the Leader's mind;
the dream had not caused him to wake up sweating, nor
afraid, the dream was not to be misunderstood as a side
effect of intestinal gases erupting in the sleeping brain; the
dream was timely; dreams of this nature were common in
the lives of chosen men, prophets and the like; the dream
emanated from the greater Arab subconscious – it was
a token of truth, a revelation. After five hours of intense
exegesis, the Council voted unanimously that the dream
was to be acted upon as the Leader saw fit. The Leader was
displeased; not one of the 'sons of whores' – as he called
them – had understood the meaning of the dream. The room
grew smaller. A line of warrior ants trickled out from a
loose tile on the wall. One of the Councillors fainted and
was carried away. The Leader lit a long – Cohiba Lancero
– cigar and an attendant unrolled a map onto the table.
What stood between the Leader's dream and reality was the
existence of this: the Leader tapped his finger onto the map.
'This!' exclaimed the Leader, tapping emphatically, was to
be taught a lesson. The meeting concluded, the six Council
members each received keys to brand new Toyota Coronas
– gifts for their relatives, wired with Stasi microphones. The
seventh – who had fainted – joined the food chain in the
artificial lake.*

*The Leader, who would not sleep now, called for his
barber. As the barber painted his white hairs black,
applied warm wax to his cheeks and restored the flush and
glow of youth to his head, the Leader picked up his large
leader's phone and called April,[2] Plenipotentiary-at-large
of the Great Player. 'I have had a dream,' he said. 'How
delightful,' she replied. She – unlike our Leader, who was a
man of the past – was a woman of the future. The certainty
of knowledge given to her by this curious birthright meant
that during her exchanges with him, she neither appeased
him, nor was at any time duped into giving explicit consent
to what would later be called his 'tyrannical madness', his
'consummate evil' and 'terrorist designs'. She knew what to
say and what to do; April knew what was what.*

*At noon on the following day, April and the Leader sat
in deep leather sofas, facing one another, with uncrossed
arms. The interpreter – Sadoun – settled precariously on
the edge of a straight-backed chair between them. 'We have
no opinion on your Arab–Arab conflicts, it's not our affair,'
said April, sprightly. The sun was pulling high as a dagger
and the phones had stopped ringing. The Leader put a long
– Cohiba Lancero – cigar between his lips and Sadoun leapt
to light it.*

*The events of the story unfolded on 25 July 1990. Eight
days later, the Leader's dream rolled across the Kuwaiti
border and the world as the writer of this tale knew it, once
again, altered forever.*

* * *

However tempting it might have been to throw the book of Western
literary evil – *Richard III* – at Saddam Hussein, this strategy could –
at best – produce a freak show. The Americans were already making
daytime reality television out of Saddam's trial. A play conceived
along the lines of the freak show could neither aspire to expiate
the sins of the region, nor reduce the likelihood of other tyrants
succeeding him.

A significant and enduring part of Shakespeare's undertaking
in the War of the Roses cycle was to conjure up the horrors of
the English civil war and, through their depiction, to expiate
them: the history cycle as dramatic exorcism of the spirit of self-
murder. However, when *Richard III* is presented as a standalone
piece and removed from the Henry VI cycle, a foreshortening of
perspective occurs and a distorting emphasis falls on Richard's
individual psychology and personality. The context of war, cyclical
violence and relentless brutalization of society is marginalized and
overlooked. Richard of Gloucester appears as if he were a self-
generated phenomena, an agent – not a by-product – of history.
As a result, his actions are reduced into a mere – though brilliant –
spectacle of evil. We are attracted by Richard's relentless energy and
the compelling, voyeuristic thrill of watching Vice strut, curse, dare
and conquer, but we are never invited to perceive Richard's ruthless

criminality as a result and consequence of what came before him. Richard is removed from historical causality and we are absolved of an understanding of historical agency. All we can do is hiss, boo and watch agog as he murders his way through the ranks of society.

To make a coherent approximation of Richard III and Saddam Hussein one would need to go to the roots of this twentieth-century tyranny, commencing with tracing history that precedes Saddam's rise to power by at least 50 years: the collapse of the Ottoman Empire, the imposition by the British of the Hashemite line of King Faisal, the military coup of Abdul Kareem Qassim, the hanging of bodies on lampposts, the Ba'athization of society, the police state, the rampant networks of secret services, spies and informers, the Iran–Iraq war, his quasi-deification by the Sunni Muslim Gulf States, the West's declared support for Iraq and covert support of Iran, the invasion of Kuwait, the embargo, and on and on. Layer upon layer of history.

Anything less than this, particularly in the context of the cross-cultural circumstances of this piece, would be to promote a reductive – and reactionary – equivalence between supreme moral evil and Arab-ness. Richard's characteristic vitality, sexual potency, wit, charm are the same tropes that suffuse the Western Orientalist fantasy of the Arab tyrant; the combination would not convey the nature of evil in a general sense, rather it would convey the nature of evil *Arabs*. It would ineluctably feed Western audiences' worst prejudices about Arabs in general. The conflation of the familiar story of the bottled spider with the – less familiar but highly media-tized – tale of the Butcher of Baghdad was a dangerous and toxic red herring.

Yes, it would be a riot of self-satisfied Western gloating at the cruelty of the hook-nosed Arab; indeed, it would be a fabulous blood-fest in which the Allah wallah hajjis are paraded on stage, ripping each other's throats out, whilst discreetly obeying the hymn sheet of an English History play! It's doubtful this Arab Richard would even require a physical deformity – his ethnicity would suffice. 'Arab' would carry the full designation of the curse of nature and the production could save on a hump! Most damning of all, it would be as if the American Occupation of Iraq never took place and the writer/adaptor and his troupe of actors would be feted in Western capitals as the unsuspecting minstrels of the New World Order. His experience as the Arab 'voice' in Tokyo, London and other fine cities had taught him that inter-cultural 'forums' accompany, as do valets their masters, the real wars that surrounded him. There was more dignity, he mused – and theatricality – in Muntadhar Al Zaidi's shoe, unceremoniously chucked at George Bush's head during a press conference in Baghdad, shouting, 'Taste your farewell kiss from the people of Iraq, you dog!'

* * *

But *Richard III* is also a play about the nature of kingship. As the writer's wife – and dramaturge – pointed out, the court intrigues, the tribal affiliations, the internal factionalism, the in-fighting of the play were reminiscent, above all, of the day-to-day life of the ruling Gulf monarchies. The more he moved away from the notion of transposing the play into the context of Iraq, the more engaging this aspect of the play became.

Underpinning the theme of kingship is the question of legitimacy. The lion's share of Richard and Buckingham's plotting is concerned with overcoming Richard's illegitimacy and the legalistic barriers between him and the throne. The murder of Clarence and the infanticide of the young princes; the manipulation of popular support to buttress Richard's claim in the Lord Mayor's scene; all evidence a recognized, natural pattern of succession that needed systematically subverting. The legal structures governing succession and kingship needed to be destroyed and hijacked. A crisis of monarchical succession is, by and large, an anachronistic issue for the democracies of the developed world. The Arabian Gulf, however, is not – politically – part of the developed world and nowhere is the fear around monarchical succession more acute than in the contemporary Gulf Arab petro-states. The nightmare scenario runs like this: the incumbent King dies and no clear succession is in place – or illness impedes the nominal Crown Prince from assuming their duties. A power vacuum ensues that brings the unreconciled factions from the ruling clan into direct confrontation. The resultant conflagration would have the scope and virulence of an all-consuming power struggle that would, it's feared, rip society apart along tribal, sectarian and ethnic fault lines. Failing outside intervention, civil war is the most likely outcome. This is the unspoken twenty-first-century nightmare of these monarchies.

On his way back from a casting trip to Damascus, on the front page of the *Al Hayat* newspaper, the writer read of the establishment of the Council of Allegiance. The ageing incumbent King of Saudi Arabia created the Council of Allegiance to ensure the smooth transition of power in the event of incapacitation or death of the (future) King or Crown Prince. To a mind obsessed with Richard of Gloucester, and the 'princely heap' that surrounds him, the Council's criteria for the selection of rulers read like an invitation to unmolested villainy:

• Support within the Al Saud (the ruling family).
• Tenure in government.
• Tribal affiliations and origins of a candidate's mother.
• Religious persona.
• Acceptance by the Ulema (leaders of the religious establishment).
• Support by the merchant community.
• Popularity among the general Saudi citizenry.

Richard III then, neither as a journey into the pathology of evil, nor as the portrait of a spent Arab tyrant, but as a foray and impromptu around a very real threat: a power vacuum inside a contemporary tribal, petro-monarchy. Here, finally, was a reading that rendered the material both radically contemporary and highly subversive.

Frontal criticism of Gulf monarchs is illegal; it is a state security offence. This was no joke. To take a composite, non-specified, 'Gulf monarchical family' as the direct allegorical referent of the play and to put the characters on stage in realistic costumes, language and settings meant that the adaptive strategies pursued with the text itself had to be both carefully thought out and economical. The body armour provided from the censor's whip by the Shakespeare label could be moved around the body but not removed entirely. Only through a pronounced fidelity to the outer structure of the ancient, revered – and ostensibly harmless – Shakespearean text would it be possible to deflect the probing eye of both the critic and the censor. The characters would need to maintain their Shakespearean names;

location names – for instance, Pomfret palace – could be allowed to morph into generic names, like the 'Main Square', but there was little to be gained from forcing any further geographical specificity. Divergences from the original had to be surgically placed.

These measures of self-censorship were a small price to pay for the unleashing of the material. Given that the play was to be performed in Arabic and hence, *a priori*, unleashed from the letter of the original text, the space for contemporary allusion created by the multiple registers of Arabic – dialect, colloquial, Qur'anic, classical – was infinite. Geography, for instance, could be inferred from choice of vocabulary. Social status, level of education and even the origins of a character's mother could be implied by language. Thus it was that Richard's opening monologue was developed with a poet[3] skilled in Bedouin poetry, which immediately made Richard stand out from the linguistic register used by his brothers, who employed a more urbane, courtly, vanilla Arabic. Margaret's language was littered with ancient, tribal metaphors, elements of her curses taken from Mesopotamian laments, as old as the delta. Suddenly, the play was not about history, or paying lip service to a world classic; it became an action painting that depicted a thrillingly actual or near-future meltdown scenario with all the dizzying plethora of detail and possibilities that came with that. From here, Buckingham could become a Levantine Arab advisor working for Gulf Arab monarchs and spying for Western interests. From here, one could legitimately populate the imaginary landscape with American ambassadors, feuding princes, immigrant workers, fabulous wealth, extreme entitlement and the price of crude oil.

The architecture was now in place to allow the play to become a crucible of internal, domestic political tensions in the Gulf region whilst, simultaneously, acting as a mirror for the political expediency of the Western states. The play was set to carry a double charge, able to address audiences on both sides of the cultural divide with sufficient urgency and power to unsettle both.

He'd found the way forward: Richard as the nightmare scenario of Gulf monarchies. Music, costume, props and even language – dialect – were made to embellish this imaginary world. From this point on, there was no turning back.

* * *

In making a piece about rulers and tyranny in the Middle East, it's difficult to assess the kind of impact it might have on rulers themselves. In the touring life of the piece, there was more than one occasion that it held a mirror up to nature. A brilliant, picaresque account of the touring life of this piece is contained in the documentary film, *Richard III: 'An Arab VIP'*,[4] which follows a portion of the troupe's tour to the United States and the United Arab Emirates.

In late May 2008 the ambassador of a Western diplomatic mission in Damascus sent an internal communiqué. In it, the ambassador relates the curious and grotesque evening when the Syrian President, Bashar Al Assad, unexpectedly presented himself at the performance of *Richard III, an Arab Tragedy*. In so far as this note reveals how intimately theatre and power are interlinked in the Arab world and offers a wry, Wikileak-ean insight into the nature of international perceptions, it is included below.

> Subject: Arab Shakespeare – Bashar al Assad, *Richard III*
> and the shadow of Samir Kassir.
> Résumé: Actors on stage, characters in the audience.
> As part of Damascus Capital of Culture 2008, the Opera
> House presented *Richard III* in a very special production
> by Sulayman Al Bassam. Small auditorium (200–300
> seats). The second night, Friday 16 May, Bashar Al Assad
> attended the play in the company of his wife and a reduced
> entourage, consisting of a handful of bodyguards. The
> curator of the festival and the Director of the Opera were
> informed of his visit at the last moment. The audience (of
> which I was a part, but that consisted primarily of students)
> were not expecting the President to attend: what we knew
> was that Al Bassam had recycled Shakespeare's text (in
> Arabic) to make a devastating denunciation of modes of
> government in contemporary Arab states. Some spectators
> (that rare brand of opposition intellectuals not in prison)
> refused to stand up upon the arrival of the Presidential
> couple, as custom dictates.

Did the President know what he was about to see?
Opinions vary. Bashar was visibly taken aback by the décor
of the play, in which the central element was an oversized
portrait of the sovereign of the fictitious state in which the
play unfolds (the portrait collapses in the opening moments
of the play). Along with the rest of the audience, he laughed
when Richard's councillors pleaded with him to take the
throne, arguing an internet survey proves that he has the
support of 'Ninety-nine per cent of the population'. He was
amused by the references to Ban Ki-Moon and Amr Moussa.
He seemed untroubled by the fierce satire levelled at the
Muslim religion. He did, however, give the impression of
being less and less relaxed as the piece approached its end
– the last part presents the American ambassador extending
support to Richard's ex-partisans, turned rebels. In one of the
final moments, an actor reads out a list of 'martyrs' who died
under tyranny, in which appears the name of Samir Kassir –
a leading Lebanese intellectual, assassinated in a car bomb
attack.

In brief – the actors were on the stage and the characters
of the play were in the audience, the phantoms summoned
by the play were by no means fantastical. Curious choice,
then, for Bashar (Al Assad) to expose himself to this story of
lawless, internecine and bloody struggle for power between
members of the same family. Philosophically speaking, one
may speculate that the President took cathartic pleasure from
the piece, even though, as one of his courtiers told me, the
President was quite furious at the mention of Samir Kassir
(he left without congratulating the actors or the director,
which is against his habit).

Politically, assuming that the President knew – more or
less – what he was coming to see, there's a certain courage
to publicly show himself contemplating – via the distorting
mirror of Shakespeare's genius – the woes of the people of
the Middle East and the turpitudes of their rulers. Unless of
course the explanation is much simpler and that, failing in
this as they do in other things, Bashar's services had simply

failed to brief him correctly on the tenor and content of this *Richard III, an Arab Tragedy*.

Nor, we might add, is it impossible that Bashar Al Assad attended the play, as did the Virgin Queen, in the prosaic expectation of discovering a new paean to his own infinite glory.

Notes

1　Awni Karoumi, Iraqi dramaturge, teacher, director and friend, 1945–2006.
2　April Glaspie, 13th US ambassador to Iraq. Further details of Ambassador Glaspie's meeting with Saddam Hussein can be found in Wikileaks Cables, (http://wikileaks.org/cable/1990/07/90BAGHDAD4237.html). In this cable, following one of Saddam's monologues, we read the following jewel of diplomatic understatement and Husseinian theatrics, 'At this point', writes Ambassador Glaspie, 'the Interpreter and one of the Notetakers broke down and wept.'
3　Mahdi Al Sayigh.
4　*Richard III: 'An Arab VIP'*, documentary feature, directed by Shakir Abal and Tim Langford, The Culture Project, 2009.

Richard III, an Arab Tragedy

The play was commissioned by the Royal Shakespeare Company as part of the Complete Works Festival, 2007 and first performed at The Swan Theatre, Stratford-upon-Avon on 8 February 2007.

Note on Text: *Unlike the other two texts in the trilogy that were free adaptations of and improvisations on the original, composed in English; this version of Richard III was reworked directly in Arabic and is much closer to the original. What you read here is a translation of the Arabic performance text.*

Note on costume: *The characters in their appearance need to resemble as closely as possible the entourage and ruling elites of the Gulf Arab states. State-specific and other local variants on this theme need to be resolved to avoid the costume citing any one particular state, unless this is the desired direction of the production. Buckingham and Mr Richmond should, however, be dressed in distinctly Western attire; suits and ties.*

The ruling brothers

Emir Gloucester – *Minister of Interior, then King*
Emir Clarence – *A religious man*
King Edward – *A profligate ruler*

The women

Margaret – *A dispossessed Queen*
Elizabeth – *A Queen, then a survivor*
Anne – *A victim, then a Queen*
Shore – *A palace courtesan*

The courtiers

Hastings – *An oligarch and Minister of State*
Lord Mayor – *An oligarch and Hastings' twin*
Buckingham – *A palace advisor and spy*
Rivers and Grey – *Elizabeth's cousins, soft-skinned Princes*
Stanley – *A noble soul*
Catesby – *An apparatchik*
Ratcliffe – *Catesby's nephew*
Young Prince Edward – *The legitimate Crown Prince*
A television presenter

The outsiders

Mr Richmond – *Diplomatic envoy of a foreign superpower*[1]

Other characters

A woman, Um Khaled
A murderer

(The hum of central air-conditioning, the dry rattle of ducts, should accompany the internal scenes.)

Prelude

(Hanging above the stage an oversized portrait of a former Ruler, printed on cloth. Visible momentarily, as **Margaret** *enters, the portrait collapses and* **Margaret** *retrieves it from the floor.)*

Margaret   I am Margaret. You needn't be concerned about me; we lost. It is your right to ignore me. I would ignore myself if my history let me. I don't want your loans, your gifts, your reconstruction grants; I don't want your pity – we lost. All I ask from you is not to question my thirst for revenge. It's not because I'm Arab, I read history and see. In all events, my name is not Margaret but our history is so awful, even the victors have changed their names. *(Exit* **Margaret** *singing an old Syriac death song.)*

Article One

Scene One, the palace

Sounds of a raucous party in the background.

Richard   *(Holding a pen and a paper file.)*
The earth has changed its skin,
the cold bite of metal given way to the lazy warmth of spring;
War's too fat for armour, too drunk to roar
War's a shaven testicle in Olga's scented paw.

Grizzly brother Akhwans[2] who waged the valiant fight
are clean-whiskered now, soft-skinned,
loose-jawed on Armani beds,
oiling whisper lusts with Snafi[3] screams.

Buckingham*, seated in a surveillance room, taps the following message into an electronic device.*

Dear R, Party again tonight, 3rd in three days. E. on drip by day, Viagra by night – not long now. Sound attached, Yours, B.

Richard   But I, whose chest is weighed with a weather-proof heart,
Shorn of a mug to lock the lusty female eye;
I, born to the mother with the narrow pelvis,
spat into this world so beaten, buckled and battered that even maids start at me.
No lover I; but plots I have laid
to set my brother Clarence and the King in deadly enmity. And if King Edward be as true and just
as I am subtle and treacherous then Clarence will be imprisoned because of a prophecy, which says that 'G'
will be the murderer of Edward's heirs.
If Generals can drive the world to war with Powerpoint,
Cannot Richard reduce it to ashes with a few boxes of semtex
and a gaggle of hooded pamphleteers?
Dive, thoughts, into my files: here comes Clarence.

*Enter **Clarence**, long-bearded, wearing the shortened garb of Islamic piety. He carries a file – his arrest warrant.*

Good morning, brother. What does this file mean?

Clarence   It's the warrant for my arrest.

Richard   Why?

Clarence   Because of my name.

Richard   Your name?

Clarence   See how far our brother has drifted into delirium and heresy. He plucked the letter 'Geem' from the consonants and claims that a witch prophesied that 'Geem' will disinherit his children. As my name begins with 'Geem', it follows in his thought that I am he.

Richard   It's not the King that sends you to the Tower. This is the work of women! Your suffering is spawned in the Queen's head: Elizabeth! She sent the Minister of State to the basements and now she wants the King's brothers there too!

Clarence   She rips and she sews.

Richard   We are not safe Clarence, we are not safe.

Clarence   We are not. Last night I dreamt we were fishing together in the Gulf, you stumbled and struck me overboard. Oh God! What pain it was to drown!

We hear an Arabian Gulf sea shanty, 'O ya maal'.

Richard   And you a man of God.

Clarence   Then I saw the figure of a child dabbled in blood. He cried out: 'Clarence is come. False Clarence – the coward that ran the knife between my child-thin ribs. Seize him Fires of Hell, make him taste the torment!'

Richard   Say no calamity will strike us other than what has been decreed.

Clarence   God alone can free me from torment.

Richard   What about me?! I'll deliver you or take your place in that underground hell. Have patience.

Clarence   It is God's will and there is none that can oppose Him.

Exit **Clarence**.

Richard   *(To himself.)* Gods don't share designs with mules!

Enter **Catesby** *and* **Hastings**.

Hastings   Good day to you, Emir!

Richard   And to you, Minister. *(To* **Catesby**.*)* Catesby.

Catesby   Morning, sir.

Richard   A faithful lad that one; asked about you every day.

Hastings   He's long been my boy.

Richard   How did your Excellency brook imprisonment?

Hastings   With patience, but I shall live to pay back my enemies.

Richard   No doubt and so shall Clarence; your enemies are now his, too.

Hastings   The head sleeps and the tails do wag.

Richard   Mosquitoes in our lands become hawks!

Hastings   Meat-eating rabbits!

Catesby   For want of stallions, we saddle hounds.

Gloucester *has taken Hastings' hand, conspiratorially. They whisper as* **Buckingham** *listens through headphones to their conversation.*

Hastings   There are many across the region who would dearly love to see the end of her.

Richard   There are many at home.

Hastings   The Generals–

Richard   I know.

Hastings   And if you were to put your hand in mine, Richard, we could–

They lean towards each other, whisper inaudibly, shake hands and break.

Hastings   The King?

Richard   Weak. His physicians fear his star is waning.

Hastings   There is no power but Allah's. It's his hunger for women that has brought him to this – filthy!

Richard   Very grievous.

Hastings   It tires body and soul.

Catesby   Not yours! I've got Shore lined up for you – she's worth three.

Hastings   Shh! Is the King in his bed?

Richard   He is. Go on and I'll follow.

Exit **Hastings** *and* **Catesby***, who is surreptitiously tipped by* **Richard***.*

Richard   He cannot live but must not die till Clarence is sent to heaven. *(Hears* **Anne's** *lamentations, off.)* Ah! Lancaster's youngest daughter – well, why not? Granted, I killed her husband and his father. The readiest way to make the wench amends is to become her husband and her father; not for love but for a reason buried in Jacob's soul, which I must reach unto.

Scene Two, the mourning

Anne *enters, dressed in black, followed by a score of females. A female azza (mourning ceremony) is established in which women offer condolences to the widow and mourn the bereaved communally. Disguised in black abbayas (veils),* **Richard** *and* **Catesby** *join the line of female mourners and sit beside* **Anne***.*

Anne   May Allah's curses fall on the hand that punctured your flesh, on the heart that pierced your heart and the blood that spilt your blood. Should your murderer marry, may misery be his wife's lot. And if he should bring forth a child may it come to life twisted, premature and deformed.

Richard   *(In a whisper.)* I'm so sorry.

Anne   *(In a whisper.)* Devil! Trouble us not!

Richard   Don't make a scene! Allow me, divine perfection of a woman, to acquit myself of slanders amassed around my name.

Anne   Infection of a man, there is no slander, only fact!

Richard   Fairer than tongue can name you–

Anne   Fouler than heart can think you!

Richard   I did not kill your husband.

Anne   Oh! He's alive, then!

Richard   No, he is dead.

Anne   This former Ruler – did you not murder him?!

Richard   I grant you.

Anne   Grant me, dog! *(Publicly.)* O, He was gentle mild and virtuous!

Richard   *(Publicly.)* So like the angels that have him now!

Anne   *(In a whisper.)* He's in heaven, where you will never reach.

Richard   *(In a whisper.)* Let him thank me, by our hand he enjoys the fruits of paradise.

Anne   You are only fit for hell.

Richard   I am fit for one place other.

Anne   Some dungeon.

Richard   Your bed! Your beauty was the cause of my crime; it haunted me in my sleep and led me to undertake the death of all the world to repose one little hour on your full breast. He that killed your husband did it to help you to a better husband.

Anne   There is no better on this earth.

Richard   He lives that wants you more than him.

Anne   Where?

Richard   Here! *(***Richard*** reveals himself.* ***Anne*** *spits in his face.)*

Women at wake.
Nadine Joma'a, Monadhil Daood, Fayez Kazak. Photo by Ellie Kurtz.

Richard   Rose water! Again. *(Pandemonium erupts in the mourning ceremony;* **Catesby** *wields a whipping cane to subdue the terrorized women.)*

Anne   Your sight infects my eyes.

Richard   Your eyes have bewitched mine. I am your slave. I worship you in my prayers and waking. *(Offering her his pistol.)* Take the gun – kill me. Death is sweet that comes from your hand. Don't hesitate; I did kill your father-in-law but your beauty provoked me to it. Kill me! I killed your young husband but your eyes forced me to it. *(***Anne** *drops the pistol.)* Pick it up, or take my hand.

Anne   Enough, hypocrite. I cannot kill you, though I want you dead.

Richard   Tell me to kill myself and I'll do it.

Anne   I did!

Richard   In a fit of rage, speak it again.

Anne   If I could only know your heart.

Richard   It's drawn on my tongue.

Anne   I fear both are false.

Richard   Then no tongue on earth is true!

Anne   Pick up your gun.

Richard   Say your slave is forgiven.

Anne   Not now.

Richard   Have mercy, then, on your slave and wear this ring.

Anne   *(Taking the ring.)* To take is not to give.

Richard   Look how the ring encompasses your finger: even so your breast encloses my poor heart and both are yours.

Richard *draws her to him to kiss her, but their action is interrupted by the call to prayer.*

Catesby   Prayer time, women – clear off!

Catesby *liberally distributes money to the women; some keep it, whilst others throw the money at* **Anne***'s feet, in disgust.*

Richard   A parting word?

Anne   Imagine it's been said.

Exit **Anne***.*

Richard   Was ever woman in this humour wooed? Was ever woman in this humour won?
By God, I've underestimated myself all these years.
This pert-bosomed beauty sees in me a clean-whiskered, soft-skinned lover.
I'll tint my hair with henna, douse kohl upon my eyes,
Summon an army of tailors to study my forms.
Shine out my sun, shine out.

Richard *exits, crooning a Khaleeji (Gulf Arab) love song.*

Scene Three, the palace

Rivers   Have patience, madam; the King will recover his health!

Elizabeth   What's my fate if he dies?

Rivers   No worse fate than the loss of such a great man.

Elizabeth   If the eye is blind, what's the good of light?

Rivers   God has blessed you with a fine son to comfort you when he is gone.

Elizabeth   The boy is young and his affairs are put into the hands of the Uncle, who loves neither me, nor any of you.

Grey   Is it concluded?

Elizabeth   Yes, Richard! Richard is the boy's legal guardian from the moment one of his doctors, advisors, brothers or any one of the thousand-headed staff spits poison into his gaping mouth!

Rivers and Grey   May Allah give him long life.

All   Amen.

Enter **Buckingham** *and* **Stanley**.

Buckingham   Amen. Good day, your Majesty!

Elizabeth   The King, Stanley?

Stanley   Advisor Buckingham and I are just come from visiting him.

Elizabeth   The King, Stanley!

Stanley   Have faith, madam; the King's in excellent health.

Buckingham   The King wants to re-knit the bonds of love between the Emir Richard and your brothers, your brothers and the Minister of the State Hastings – he's called a family meeting.

Elizabeth   I fear what is hidden, not manifest. I fear our happiness is at its height.

Enter **Gloucester**, **Hastings**, *followed by* **Catesby**.

Richard   They slander me – I will not suffer it!

Stanley   Hastings, you're back!

Richard   Who is it that insinuates to the King that I love them not? Is it because I cannot flatter and creep, smile, grease and pretend, nor duck with French courtesy?

Buckingham   *Politesse oblige.*

Richard   Because of this must I be held a rancorous enemy by the rabble scum of filth, liars and hypocrites?

Rivers   To whom do you address your words?

Richard   To you, rag of low birth! When have I offended you or any of your faction?

Elizabeth   Brother Richard, you mistake the matter. The King sent for you and was not provoked by anyone else. He aims at your interior hatred against my kindred and myself.

Richard   Who's to say? The world's grown so bad that sparrows are made to molest eagles.

Elizabeth   You envy the advancement of my circle. May Allah grant we never have need of you!

Richard   God grant me the same! You are the cause of my brother Clarence's imprisonment and other stains on the nobility–

Elizabeth   I swear I never provoked his Majesty against Clarence; I'm his most earnest advocate.

Richard   And do you deny that you were the cause of Hastings' imprisonment?

Rivers   She may deny it, sir.

Richard   She may, Master Rivers, she may do more; she may help you to many high advancements and then deny her hand therein–

Elizabeth   I have too long borne your blunt upbraidings and bitter scoffs – the river has broken its banks!

I shall acquaint his Majesty with the taunts I've endured.

Richard   What! Threaten me with the King's rod, will you? Tell him; don't hide a hair! It's time to speak.
Before you were Queen, nay, before your husband was King, I was the motor in his machine, the sword of his will! I spilt my blood–

Rivers   We all spilt our blood!

Hastings   When?

Rivers   When I brought you the Crown Prince!

Hastings   Liar!

Richard   During that time you and your *late* husband were sided with the tribe of Lancaster.

Elizabeth   You are opening the seams of sedition!

Hastings   Buckingham, open the archives!

Richard   Let me remind you what you were and what you are: what I was and what I am.

Rivers   In those turbulent times we followed our lawful King, as we would follow you, if you were our king.

Richard   Your King? I'd rather be a peddler in the souk.

Elizabeth   May Allah never show us that day.

Richard   I'd rather be a refugee in Shatila!

Elizabeth   May you drink from the bitter cup that I have drunk from!

Enter **Margaret***, carrying a suitcase.*

Margaret   Thieves! That fight over what you have pillaged from me! Though you do not kneel as my subjects because I'm no longer your Queen, yet fear runs in your veins because you know yourselves illegitimate!

Richard   Foul, filthy witch, weren't you banished on pain of death?

Margaret   Death is sweeter than to live a scabied camel in exile. *(To* **Richard***.)* A husband and a son are debts around your neck; *(To* **Elizabeth***.)* and a Kingdom around yours. My sorrows are yours and all your usurped pleasures are mine.

Richard   This is my father's curse when you dabbed his brows in his son's innocent blood. God plague you.

Elizabeth   Allah grants justice and does not forget.[4]

Hastings   To wrongdoers, wrong is done.

Rivers   Allah will not forgive your sins.

Margaret   You were snarling like wolves when I came and now you turn your hatreds on me? Can curses pierce the clouds and enter heaven? Then give way dull clouds to my quick curses! If not by war, then by excess die your King as ours by murder was removed to make him King! *(To* **Elizabeth***.)* May thy son, the Crown Prince, die violently in his prime in payment for my son who was the Crown Prince,

And may this debt be ripped from your flesh,
You who are the Queen for me who was the Queen.
And may your life be longer than you can endure bewailing it
and see another stand proud in your place as I see you now
trembling in mine!
Rivers and Hastings! You who stood by when my son was
shredded into ribbons by knives;
I pray Allah your lives be prematurely cut by the blade of your
sins!

Richard   She done, the hell hag?

Margaret   Stay, dog! Listen to me, you promiscuous pig, you
stain of Fate! You shame of your mother's womb! You loathed
issue of your father's loins, you stained rag of honour, you foul,
detested–

Richard   Margaret.

Margaret   Let me finish my curse!

Richard   I did it for you; it ends in 'Margaret'.

The assembled laugh. **Margaret**, *ridden by a spasm of rage, tries
to attack* **Gloucester**, *but is prevented by the courtiers. She begins
to moan.*

Richard   This is the djinn inside her: remove it! Beat her! The
devil inside her is a horse! Catesby, ride the djinn!

The males beat **Margaret** *with their Iqals.*[5]

Elizabeth   Thus your curse returns against yourself.

Margaret   Poor painted queen! *(She draws* **Gloucester** *to her
and places her lips on his forehead.)* May each of you live as the
subjects of his hate and he to yours: may this be Margaret's curse
on you.

Exit **Margaret**.

Richard   Can't blame her, she's had it hard and I repent of any
hand I had in her suffering.

Elizabeth   I swear I have always shown her due respect.

Richard   Yes and Clarence had his share of your due respect, too. (*The Queen is ushered out by* **Rivers** *and* **Grey**.) Allah pardon them that are the cause of it! *(**Hastings** and **Stanley** exit.)*

Catesby   Allah pardon them … *(**Richard** tips him.)*

Richard   *(On mobile telephone.)*
Hello my little man? The warrant yes, well done. Be sudden. Clarence speaks honey words, I fear they'll soften your heart. Your eyes drop stones. Go to it, son.

Buckingham, *seated in a surveillance room, taps the following message into an electronic device.*

Dear R, Hastings out in a puke green bisht. Margaret mad and prowling – no threat. Richard publicly accused Elizabeth of Clarence imprisonment. Sound attached, Yours, B.

Scene Four, the prison

Clarence *enters with a suitcase, identical to* **Margaret's**. *He opens it flat on the ground, and uses the water inside it to make ablutions in preparation for prayer.*

Clarence   I swear there is no God but Allah. God forgive my sins. *(Enter* **Murderer**.) In God's name, what are you?

Murderer   A man, as you are.

Clarence   If you be hired for money go back again and I will send you to my brother, the Emir Richard. He shall reward you better for my life than the King does for news of my death.

Murderer   You are deceived: he hates you.

Clarence   Do not slander him. He is kind and merciful.

Murderer   Merciful as rain on mud huts. He sent me to slaughter you. Pray now for you must die.

Clarence   Dare you counsel me to pray to God yet would war with God by murdering me? He who kills without due reason, it is as though he kills the whole of humanity.[6]

Murderer   Pray!

Clarence   And do not shed blood that is sacred by Allah's law.[7]

Murderer   Pray!

Clarence   Al Rawandi, in the sources says: 'beware of shedding innocent blood'–

Murderer   Pray! Pray!

The Murderer drowns him in the case of water. We hear an Arabian Gulf sea shanty, 'O ya maal'. **Buckingham**, *seated in a surveillance room, taps the following message into an electronic device.*

R.- Clarence removed from the game. Blow to moderate Islamic bla bla. No blowback anticipated. Yours, B.

Article Two

Scene One, the palace

King Edward   Allah bless our deeds and grant our efforts success. Brothers; I want you to build on this bond of unity, to be like one hand, to be like the hunting dog that faithfully brings the prey to the master; to be like the palm: tall and strong. The palm is blessed, it gives us dates and date juice which is a fine digestive but do not over-consume it, brothers, it ruins your teeth and will give you the shits. *(***Elizabeth*** whispers to him.)* Yes, as the woman reminds me I want you to be like a majestic structure, each part sustaining the other! Brothers, my days are numbered.

All   Allah give you long life!

King Edward   I want you now to swear before me your allegiance to me in love and duty. *(To* **Rivers***.)* You – the salty one – you start!

Rivers   Swear? By God, I will! Hastings being my senior should, of course, swear first but he's just out of, well–

Hastings   Where? Go on say it!

Grey   I'll say it: prison!

A scuffle erupts between **Hastings** *and* **Grey**.

King Edward   What is this chaos? 'Obeisance of your elders is like obeisance of God, if only man kneweth it is a great oath.' Thus said God! *(To* **Elizabeth***.)* And you, woman! I don't exempt you from my warning! Nor your idiot nephew, nor this advisor. What's his name?

All   Buckingham!

King Edward   You were all factious and riddled with enmity until I united you!

Hastings   I swear, your Majesty, to forget all our former hatreds.

Elizabeth   So do I, Hastings, swear to bury old enmity.

Buckingham   May Allah's curses fall on me if I carry towards you or your tribe any hatred.

King Edward   Well done. Now let's have a photo. *(To* **Buckingham***.)* You, the Frenchie! *(Enter* **Richard***.)* Emir Richard, we have made peace of enmity and fair love of hate between these in-fighting brothers.

Richard   A blessed labour, my King. Should anyone here by false intelligence hold me a foe, I desire to reconcile myself in peace. First, madam, I entreat true peace of you and will purchase it with my true services. Buckingham, if ever any grudge were lodged between us and you Rivers; indeed of you all. I do not know anyone in the Arab world with whom my soul is any jot at odds. Photo, Frenchie!!

Elizabeth   I beseech your Majesty in this blessed hour to utter your pardon for our brother Clarence.

King Edward   Dutiful wife!

Richard   Have I offered my love to be so bouted in this royal presence? Who knows not that Clarence is dead? *(Throwing a file onto the floor.)*

Rivers   Who knows not he is dead, who knows he is?

Elizabeth   All-seeing heaven what a world is this!

Richard   You mock his corpse, madam.

Kind Edward   Is Clarence dead?

Richard   Allah rest his soul.

King Edward   My order was reversed.

Richard   But he by your first order died. Allah's will and nothing can refute it. And it is Allah's will that others who deserve worse than he remain beyond suspicion.

Enter **Stanley***, flustered.*

Stanley   Your Majesty, I will not rise till you grant me my request!

King Edward   Speak Stanley, what is it?

Stanley   In a fit of drunkenness my Bangladeshi killed a driver and–

King Edward   Shut up! It was a word from a broken, sapless King that killed my brother and now you want a word to pardon one of your servants? Which one of you spoke on Clarence's behalf? Which one of you reminded me of him! O God, I fear your vengeance will take hold of me. I don't want to see your faces. Hastings, take me away.

Exit all except **Richard** *and* **Buckingham**.

Richard   This is the fruit of rashness! Did you mark how guilty pale the kindred of the Queen looked when they heard of Clarence's death? They forced the King to it. But Allah's hand is mighty and vengeful! The King is calling.

Buckingham   I wait upon your grace.

Buckingham *and* **Richard** *exit together.* **Edward** *dies, reported visually through a tableau or by sound. We read the following message from* **Buckingham**.

R. Edward bye. Zero hour. Moved on Richard. Later, B.

Scene Two, the palace

Elizabeth   Who shall hinder me to weep, to chide my fortune, and to myself become an enemy?

Grey   From Allah we come and to Allah we return.

Elizabeth   I want to make an act of tragic violence.

Grey   There is no will than Allah's.

Elizabeth   I'll join with black despair against my soul.

Rivers   Be rational woman! Your young son is the Crown Prince, send for him forthwith to be crowned King.

Enter **Richard** *and* **Buckingham**.

Richard　Sister, have comfort. All of us have cause to wail the death of our guiding star, but tears cannot cure catastrophes.

Buckingham　May Allah accept our late King into His Mercy and welcome him into his wide heavens. In this difficult hour, I suggest we send a discreet escort to bring the Crown Prince here presently.

Rivers　Why a discreet escort?

Buckingham　For fear that a multitude would present too ready a target to enemies of the state, Clarence's disillusioned followers, or other factions that hide between us.

Richard　I trust the King has made true peace with all of us – the pact is firm and true in me.

Rivers　And in us all. Yet since the pact is so green, it should not be exposed to unnecessary duress.
Therefore I say with Buckingham that it is right so few should escort the Prince.

Hastings　And so say I.

Richard　So be it. Madam, will you chair the meeting that decides the members of this royal escort?

Exit all but **Buckingham** *and* **Richard**.

Buckingham　Whoever goes to collect the Prince, let's not be left behind and, on the way, I'll ensure the Queen's proud relatives are removed from the Crown Prince's orbit once and for all.

Richard　My other self, my counsel, my oracle, my prophet! I call you 'cousin'; sweet cousin, I am led by you as a child is led by its mother. To the meeting!

Exit.

Scene Three, a street

Enter **Catesby** *and* **Shore**.

Catesby   Your master Hastings is out of the clink today, sunshine, so you'll be taking him in hand tonight and I want all your lips and tricks busy restoring him to his former glory.

Shore   I'm not one to disappoint.

Catesby   Good girl.

Catesby *receives a call on his mobile. Enter* **Um Khaled**, *distressed.*

Um Khaled   Um Ahmed? Um Ahmed?

Shore   Morning Um Khaled.

Um Khaled   Do you know anyone who knows anyone that knows the Emir Richard?

Shore   Why? What is it?

Um Khaled   My son. They've taken him.

Shore   Yours too! Catesby! Her son, Khaled, they've taken him!

Catesby *lifts up* **Um Khaled's** *veil to see her face and lowers his eyes to see her breasts.*

Catesby   *(To* **Um Khaled***)* Your son, is it? Don't worry, dove, Catesby's your man. I'll take care of him. Come with us, now you're part of our little flock of woe!

Exit **Catesby** *and* **Um Khaled** *and* **Shore**.

Scene Four, York TV

News Reader   The King's Diwan has formed a royal escort led by the Emir Richard and the Palace Advisor Buckingham, the Emirs Rivers and Grey to bring the Crown Prince to the capital where he will be crowned as ruler of the Kingdom.

Scene Five, the palace

Elizabeth, *holding small sea shells in her hand, from which she seeks to read prophecy. Enter* **Stanley**.

Elizabeth   Stanley? Come in!

Stanley   I carry news that grieves me to unfold.

Elizabeth   How is the Crown Prince?

Stanley   Well and in health.

Elizabeth   What's your news, then?

Stanley   Your relatives, Rivers and Grey have been arrested.

Elizabeth   Who by?

Stanley   Richard and Buckingham.

Elizabeth   On what charge?

Stanley   The sum of all I can, I have disclosed.

Elizabeth   I see the downfall of our house! The tiger now has seized the gentle hind. Welcome destruction, death and massacre! I see, as in a map, the end of all.

She throws the shells and exits. **Stanley** *kneels to collect the shells and sees a terrifying vision.*

Article Three

Scene One, the palace

Enter **Prince Edward** *and* **Buckingham**.

Buckingham   Welcome Crown Prince to your palace.

Prince Edward   Where's my mother?

Enter **Richard**.

Richard   Welcome, my brother's son and my soul's passion.

Prince Edward   Where's my mother?

Richard   Somewhere, I'm sure.

Prince Edward   My uncles would not have allowed this!

Richard   The untainted virtue of your years has not yet dived into the world's deceit. Those uncles were obstacles in your path, their honey words hid the poison in their hearts. May God keep you from them and from such false friends!

Prince Edward   God keep me from false friends, but they were none!

Enter **Hastings** *and* **Catesby**.

Richard   Look! The Minister of State comes to greet you.

Hastings   God bless you with happy days! *(***Catesby*** leaps menacingly towards the Prince.)* Don't be afraid, cousin, it's Catesby; he wants to kiss your hand.

Prince Edward   I thought my mother and my brother York would have met us on the way.

Hastings   They've taken asylum in the American Embassy, for reasons only God knows!

Buckingham   The shame of it! How indirect and peevish! Hastings will you persuade the Queen to send York unto his brother presently?

Hastings I've already sent my own brother, the Mayor. But the Ambassador sent him away, saying: 'You will not infringe the sanctity of the Embassy, even if you bring your entire army!'

Buckingham He is obstinate and backward and can't speak the language of the age!

Catesby 'Embassy sanctity' – eh? Bloody heretic! My Lord, let me take a bunch of my lads and we'll raid the Embassy!

Buckingham Political criminals who have tried to undermine national security seek the asylum offered by foreign embassies. The Prince has done no such thing. I've heard of men asylum seekers but never before of children. Therefore we break no law in removing him.

Richard Solution?

Catesby Raid the Embassy!

Hastings No! I'll see what I can do.

Prince Edward Quickly, Minister. *(Exit* **Hastings** *and* **Catesby**.*)*
If York comes, where shall we reside till our coronation?

Richard I suggest your Highness repose at the Tower for your best health and recreation.

Prince Edward I don't like the Tower of any place. Counsellor Buckingham – did the British build that place?

Buckingham They laid its foundations.

Prince Edward They know how to play history, those British.
They showered these lands with seeds
Strewn from the whitest gloves,
Seeds that to this day, bear man-eating fruits.
The robes of Empire grown thin,
they settle today for the tidy plunder
of gun running and pesticides.
I'll tell you what, Buckingham.

Buckingham What, my lord?

Prince Edward   If I live until I be a man, I'll win back our ancient rights in the Holy Lands, or die a soldier in the battlefield.

Richard   A born ruler!

A celebratory sound clip from the Palestinian Liberation Organization archive is played. **Richard** *and* **Buckingham** *raise the boy onto their shoulders and exit with him, victoriously.*

Scene Two, at the Foreign Embassy

Mr Richmond *and* **Elizabeth** *are watching the National Television broadcast of the Crown Prince's arrival to the capital. The broadcast is live from the palace. Tchaikovsky's* The Nutcracker Suite *accompanies the transmission, in the way of commentary. On screen we see* **Richard**, **Buckingham**, *Crown* **Prince Edward**, **Catesby** *and armed members of the Royal National Guard.*

Mr Richmond   Please, Your Majesty, take a seat. We should be able to pick up their conversation in between this soup; can't bear Tchaikovsky myself – you?

Elizabeth   Where are your men, Mr Richmond?

Mr Richmond   That man in the suit there, he's one of them.

Elizabeth   And the others?

Mr Richmond   They'll be there, just not in frame.

Elizabeth   How many are they?

Mr Richmond   Three in total–

Elizabeth   Three!

Mr Richmond   Three of the best.

Elizabeth   You've sent my boys to that animal–

Mr Richmond   I assure you, your Majesty–

Elizabeth   With three men!

Mr Richmond   They're perfectly safe.

Elizabeth   They are not perfectly safe. Stop saying they are perfectly safe.

Mr Richmond   This is good, solid PR for all of you, your Highness – there's my Head of Security there – shows how the constitution is holding firm. Love the eagle on the Crown Prince's arm, very manly.

Elizabeth   It's a falcon, not an eagle.

Mr Richmond   Looks fabulous. The photographers are lapping it up.

On screen **Richard** *gives the youngest Prince, York, a ceremonial knife.*

Elizabeth   What's he doing?

Mr Richmond   They're exchanging gifts. It's perfect. Like I said, there's really no need to force a stand-off with Richard at this stage – not in your interests, not in ours, not in anyone's.

Elizabeth   What's going on?

Mr Richmond   *(To his technicians.)* Turn it up a little would you?

On screen Prince York, holding the ceremonial knife, jumps on **Richard's** *back.* **Richard's** *guards start to unhinge the young Prince, meanwhile; the American guards get involved in the unhinging. A scuffle ensues at the end of which the three American guards are shot dead. The Princes are removed from camera frame; the broadcast stops abruptly and is replaced by a football match.*

Elizabeth   No!

Mr Richmond   Ah. Oh, shit.

Elizabeth   *(In Arabic.)* My children!

Exit **Elizabeth**. *Enter* **Buckingham**. **Mr Richmond** *and* **Buckingham** *lock and tremble in a terrible embrace.* **Richmond** *exits.*

Scene Three, the palace

Buckingham   Catesby, you are deep and inward with our plans; tell me, is it an easy matter to make Hastings of our mind for the instalment of Richard on the throne?

Catesby   Not easy. Hastings loves the Crown Prince for his father's sake. Not easy at all.

Buckingham   And Stanley, what's his position?

Catesby   Where Hastings pisses, Stanley pisses.

Buckingham   Go to your master Hastings, then, Catesby and find out where he stands and summon him tomorrow to the palace to discuss the coronation. If you find him tractable to us, encourage him and show him all our reasons. If he be leaden, be so too and break off your talk. Give us notice of his inclination; tomorrow we hold *divided councils* and you shall be highly employed.

Enter **Richard**.

Richard   Catesby! Commend me to the Minister of State. *(***Gloucester*** hands* **Catesby** *a file.)* Tell him his ancient knot of dangerous adversaries tomorrow are let blood in the Main Square. Bid my friend for joy of this good news, give mistress Shore one gentle kiss the more.

Exit **Catesby**.

Buckingham   What shall we do if we perceive Hastings will not yield to our complots?

Richard   Prune his nut.
And when I'm king claim of me the oilfields of the North.
They will be yours in all their dust and rolling green.

Buckingham   I'll claim that promise at your Grace's hands.

They shake hands. Enter **Mr Richmond**, *bumbling, as if by mistake.*

Mr Richmond   Hello, sorry, I …

Buckingham   Mr Richmond: Mr Richard.

Mr Richmond   Really? I had no idea! Oh, what an honour!

Richard   Welcome. *(To **Buckingham**, who translates.)* Invite him for dinner that we may digest our plots in some form.

Buckingham   He invites you to dinner.

Mr Richmond   *(In Arabic.)* Shukran!

Richard   *(In **Mr Richmond**'s language.)* Ah, you speak Arabic, marvellous!

*Exit **Richard** laughing, followed by **Mr Richmond**, delighted, and **Buckingham**, seething.*

Scene Four, Hastings' chalet

Shore *is dancing, half-dressed.* **Catesby** *is massaging* **Hastings'** *shoulders.* **Hastings** *emits little whoops of delight.* **Hastings'** *mobile phone rings.*

Hastings   Who is it?

Messenger   A messenger from Stanley.

Hastings   In the dead of night?

Messenger   Nearly dawn, sir!

Hastings   What is it?

Messenger   My Lord says he dreamt of a wild dog's muzzle in your intestines, right? He says there are two councils being held tomorrow, right? Decisions taken at one might make you regret you attended the other, right? So he says come on, we're off north, right? To evade the danger what his soul divines, right?

Hastings   Go back to Stanley and tell him he should fuck more often, right?

Messenger   Right.

Hastings   And if you call me again at this time of night, Catesby'll chew your balls off, right?

Messenger   Right.

Catesby   Message from Richard: your soft-skinned enemies, the Queen's relatives, Rivers and Grey, today in the Main Square – execution.

Hastings   That's no sad news to me.

Catesby   Richard wants to know if your hand is still in his?

Hastings   Does he mean for the crown?

Catesby   I think he does.

Hastings   I'll see this crown of mine nipped from my shoulders before I see that crown on his head.

Catesby   I live to see the day the crown sits on this pretty bud.

Hastings'*phone rings.*

Hastings   Stanley! Frightened of the dog?!

Catesby *pays off* **Shore** *and she leaves.*

Stanley   By God, I don't like these divided councils. And the dream I had makes things worse.

Hastings   Stop worrying, you old maid. I know where I stand. We'll attend one of the councils, and our man Catesby will be in the other.

Stanley   The Queen's cousins left the capital two days ago thinking their heads were secure and where are they now? In a basement awaiting the rope. *(Pause.)* We're going to the palace, then?

Hastings   We are, we are, we are we are we are! *(Hangs up, then to* **Catesby***.)* Give me some of your sweet stuff!

Catesby *whispers a vulgar joke to* **Hastings***, they cackle loudly. Another phone call:* **Buckingham***.*

Buckingham   Guffawing at dawn, Minister? Celebrating the news from the Main Square?

Hastings   Are you going to the palace?

Buckingham   Yes, but I'm back before you.

Hastings   I think I'll stay for dinner there.

Buckingham   And supper too.

Hastings   Bon appetit!

Hastings *and* **Catesby** *exit singing.*

Scene Five, the Main Square

Rivers   I, the Emir Rivers, say to you all: today you witness a subject die for truth, duty and loyalty.

Grey   I, the Emir Grey say: God keep the Crown Prince from all the pack of you! A knot you are of damned bloodsuckers!

Catesby   Filthy, dirty, soft-skinned, clean-whiskered fucks.

Rivers *and* **Grey**   Allah is Great. Allah is Great. God save the Prince!

Catesby *executes them.*

Catesby   *(On mobile phone.)* Hello, sir? Hastings said no … That's all, sir. Anything else, sir? Done with them, sir. God keep you. *(Hangs up the call and spits.)* Bring the coffee, lad, get the cushions.

Ratcliffe   Right you are, Uncle.

Scene Six, the palace

Seated on cushions, on the floor.

Hastings   My lords, the cause why we are met is to determine of the coronation. In God's name, speak: when is the royal day?

Buckingham   Are all things fitting for that royal time?

The assassination of Rivers and Grey.
Monadhil Daood, Faisal Al-Ameeri, Bashar Abdullah
(kneeling), Amal Omran. Photo by Ellie Kurtz.

Stanley   They are and it wants but nomination.

Catesby   Tomorrow I judge a happy day.

Stanley   Who knows the Protector's mind?

Catesby   *(To* **Buckingham**.*)* We think you should soonest know his mind.

Buckingham   Me? We know each other's faces, but for our hearts; he knows no more of mine than I of yours. Nor I no more of his, than you of mine; Hastings, you and he are near in love.

Hastings   I thank his Grace but for his purpose in the coronation, I have not sounded him. But you may name the time and, on the Emir's behalf, I'll give my voice, which, I presume, he'll take in gentle part.

Enter **Richard**.

Catesby   Upon your cue!

Richard   My friends and cousins. Forgive my delay; I puffed up my pillows! I trust my absence neglects no great designs, which, by my presence, might have been concluded.

Buckingham   Had not you come upon your cue, Minister Hastings had pronounced your voice for crowning of the King.

Richard   He may! His Excellency knows me well, and loves me well.

Hastings   I thank your Grace.

Richard   Catesby, I saw good dates in the neighbouring chamber; golden tinted and excellent ripe, they drew my eye: fetch me some.

Catesby   This very instant!

Exit **Catesby**. **Ratcliffe** *pours coffee for* **Richard**.

Richard   What's your name, boy?

Ratcliffe   Ratcliffe.

Richard   Who's your father?

Ratcliffe   One of your followers and Catesby is my uncle.

Richard   Good lad, stay close to me. Buckingham! *(Aside.)* Catesby's attempts have failed with the senile goat Hastings–

Buckingham   I know, withdraw – I'll follow you.

Exit **Buckingham** *and* **Richard**. *In the event the second council is shown in a visual tableau,* **Mr Richmond** *is to be present amongst the assembled.*

Stanley   Didn't you tell me Catesby was in the other meeting? Why is he fumbling in here with us?

Hastings   First it's dreams, then it's why is he coming, why is he going? Relax, Stanley!

Enter **Catesby**.

Catesby   Where is the Protector? I was sent for these dates.

Stanley   Tomorrow is too soon. We need longer to make provisions for such an important day.

Hastings   His Excellency looks cheerfully and smooth today. I think there's never a man I've met that can less hide his love or hate than he. You know his heart by one glance at his face.

Stanley   What of his heart saw you in his face today?

Hastings   That with no man here is he offended.

Stanley   I pray God he be not.

Enter **Richard** *and* **Buckingham**.

Richard   I invoke you all: tell me what they deserve that do conspire my death with devilish plots of damned witchcraft upon my body with their hellish charms?

Hastings   The tender love I bear your Grace makes me most forward to doom the offenders. Whoever they are, they deserve death!

Richard   Then be your eyes the witness of this ill. See how I am bewitched. My body is like a blasted sapling all withered up. This is Edward's wife that by her witchcraft has thus marked me, in league with that harlot strumpet ... Shore!

Hastings   If they've done this thing ...

Richard   If! Speak you to me of 'ifs'? You degenerate face-wipe! Traitor: off with his head! Catesby, you will do it! I swear I will not dine until I see that rotten, treacherous lump roll between my feet. The rest that love me rise and follow me. *(Gives* **Catesby** *a bag of money.)*

Exit all, except **Catesby** *and* **Hastings**.

Hastings   *(To* **Catesby**.*)* What's your name, what's your father's name? Who are you? *(Patting the bag of money.)* Chopped tongues.[8]

Catesby   The Emir wants his lunch.

Catesby *seizes* **Hastings** *by the scruff of the neck and leads him off.*

Scene Seven, York TV

News Reader   The Emir Gloucester and the Minister of State Hastings along with several leading cabinet members met today to finalize arrangements for the coronation of the Crown Prince. In an amusing aside, the Emir Gloucester commented on the improved quality of dates in the Royal Palace, saying such a sign boded well for the future of the state. More details to follow in our next bulletin.

Scene Eight, the palace

Richard   Buckingham, tell me by God, how do we sink terror into their souls, prune as many heads as we need to, lock up the rest and make it all legit?

Buckingham   You kidding? I can redraw the map of the globe with my finger; invade foreign lands with a flick of the wrist; flatten countries with the cock of a brow; I can make a mockery of the judiciary; thread an axis of evil through the eye of the press; turn a democracy into a tyranny and keep it all as clean and transparent as a Security Council resolution.

Richard   I love you. But how?

Buckingham   War on Terror!

A cabaret commences with a troupe of dancing girls dressed in military fatigues, armed with star-spangled umbrellas. A game of American football is played out with **Hastings'** *head, whilst* *leaflets fall from above identifying* **Hastings** *as a threat to national security. Enter the* **Mayor**.

Buckingham   Honourable Mayor!

Richard   Mortars!

Buckingham   Car bombs!

Richard   Catesby!

Buckingham   Honourable Mayor, we sent for you–

Richard   Duck!

All *(Singing.)*
There are suicide ploys in those madrassa boys
And cells that cower in the palm of rush hour
There are enemies within, like parasites on skin
But all of the above have their luck running thin
'Cause they ain't got the wag of the dog ...
No, they ain't got the wag of the dog ...

There are bombs on the way and drones on display
Laws are being cooked, eyeballs unhooked
Bags are being filled, but nobody's been killed,
Just so we understand each other you and me, I mean, brother,
There's no ideological impurity in National Security,
I repeat, there is no impurity in National Security
They don't hit the screen – the mentally unclean –
So, let bags be filled, and the sweet earth tilled
You gotta get with the wag of the dog,
Yes, you gotta get with the wag of the dog!

(The cabaret ends as abruptly as it began.)

Catesby   *(Holding* **Hastings***' head aloft.)* Here is the head of that ignoble terrorist Hastings.

Richard   So dear I loved the man that I must weep.

Buckingham   *(Addressing the* **Mayor***.)* Can you imagine, your brother was the most deeply nested of terrorists who plotted to murder myself and the Emir in the council-house today?

Lord Mayor   My brother?

Richard   Think you we are non-believers, sir? Or that we'd proceed so rashly in this terrorist's death, but that the extreme peril of the case, the immediate danger to our lives and the manifest threat to the supreme national interests, forced us to it?

Lord Mayor   Bless your hands and your swords! May God reward you for warning false traitors from like attempts!

Richard   We didn't want him dead before you heard the traitor speak and timorously confess the manner and the purpose of his treason: that you might signify the same to the citizens.

Lord Mayor   I have no need to hear sounds from the mouth of a traitor! Your testimony, your Excellency, will more than suffice. Fear not, I'll acquaint our citizens with all your just proceedings in the name of National Security.

Buckingham   You be the witness to our intentions.

Richard   Catesby, dues. *(***Catesby** *hands* **Hastings***' severed head to the* **Mayor***. Then, tearfully.)* Our deepest condolences.

Mayor *exits.*

Richard   *(To* **Buckingham***.)* He goes towards the Main Square. Follow him and infer the bastardy of Edward's children to the people there.

Buckingham   We can't hound them through the streets, cousin; we'll go to their homes, to their beds and breakfast tables. Bring the television studio here!

Richard   Brilliant!

Buckingham   *(To* **Catesby***.)* Fetch back the Mayor, Catesby; you can play the mullah. Cousin Richard, you are distressed, you are no longer of nor for this world: take this Qur'an in your hand, look morose, deepen your voice, play with these beads and around you we'll build a very holy discourse. Catesby will lead the religious charge, you rebut with counter-arguments. But be not easily won to our request. Play the virgin's part. Plead no and take it.

A makeshift TV studio is erected, the bewildered **Mayor** *is brought back in.*

News Reader   Good evening viewers and welcome to tonight's episode of *Talk of the Nation*, in which we discuss the growing power vacuum that has crippled state institutions. We welcome his Excellency the Emir Richard and Mr Catesby.

Catesby   Shaikh Catesby.

News Reader   I do beg your pardon, Shaikh Catesby.

Catesby   Your Excellency, we ask you about your refusal to accept the reins of power and this, in reality, is the question of your troubled people.

Richard   In the name of Allah the Merciful, the Bounteous and peace onto the Sire of Messengers our Prophet and adored Muhammad (Peace be upon Him). The royal tree has left us royal fruit, which will no doubt make us happy by his reign. So I don't understand your question. As for me, as you see, I am devoted to worship and reflection upon Divinity and thanks be to God.

Catesby   You refer to the sons of Edward, but as the nation will read tomorrow in the national press the DNA of these children bears no resemblance to the DNA of their father.

Richard   Our constitution is clear and DNA is a vice.

Catesby   But the tests were conducted overseas!

Richard   Overseas is a doorway to the devil.

Catesby   Your people are begging you and have no hope other than you.

Richard   Leave me in peace and find someone else. It is better for you that I am a minister working for you than a ruler over you.

Lord Mayor   Let me remind you of the holy saying: *'If you see wrong, it is your duty to correct it!'*

All   Agreed upon by all sources.

Lord Mayor   The Prophet (Peace be upon Him) sayeth: '*If the power to govern the nation is given wrongly, then await the final hour.*'

Richard   Let the final hour toll, it is a duty upon us all.

Catesby   Quiet, please, we have a call. *(Putting his hand to his earpiece.)* 'Hello? Oh, welcome. *(Laughs.)* Oh, yes, yes, I see, I do agree, oh yes, thank you, thank you, thank you so much. Bye bye!' *(To **Richard**.)* That was the Secretary General of the Arab League!!! He begs you to accept in the interests of regional security.

Richard   Let the Secretary General of the Arab League call, my mind is made up.

Catesby   Wait, wait we have another caller, it's from very far away. *(**Catesby** speaks a broken English.)* 'Hello. Yes please. Yes please. Thanks, thanks a lot. Bye bye.' That was the Secretary General of the UN!

Richard   The UN has no business interfering with our internal affairs.

Catesby   Fine, okay, but let us look at the results of our nationwide opinion poll conducted on the internet which shows: oh, well, oh, my … God be praised!! Ninety-nine per cent of the citizens have requested you to become our ruler, meanwhile … one per cent have no access to the internet.

Lord Mayor   Or their dial-up cards have run out?

Richard   If one day a people desires to live, then Fate must answer their call.[8]

Catesby   So you accept?

Richard   When do I get crowned?

Catesby   Tomorrow.

Richard   As you will. Allah bless you all.

News Reader   That was the end of our historic episode and we bid you, dear viewers, farewell until we meet again.

They are off air.

Buckingham   I salute you: long live King Richard.

Richard   *(Lifting the chair he was seated in.)* I'll keep this chair as a memento of this occasion.

They exit cackling.

Article Four[9]

Scene One, outside the palace

Anne   Good morning, sister.

Elizabeth   I see we share the same longing to visit the Princes?

Anne   Their aunt I am in law, in love their mother.

Elizabeth   Kind sister, we'll enter all together.

Ratcliffe   I may not suffer you to visit the Princes; the King has charged the contrary.

Elizabeth   Who is the King? Who?!

Ratcliffe   I meant their Protector.

Elizabeth   May God not leave him a head to be crowned.

Anne   *(To* **Ratcliffe**.*)* You are addressing the Queen, their mother, who desires to see her children.

Ratcliffe   I am bound by oath, and therefore pardon me.

Anne   May Allah's curse fall on you and him!

Enter **Stanley**.

Stanley   *(To* **Anne**.*)* Madam, please accompany me.

Anne   Where to?

Stanley   Your husband's coronation requires that you be present in the female viewing chamber.

The sound of the percussions from the coronation ceremony builds.

Elizabeth   Cut my dress open that this heart may have some scope to beat, or else I collapse with this dead-killing news!

Anne   The flood starts with a drop.

Stanley   Come, madam, come; I was sent in haste.

Elizabeth   Go, go, Anne, I envy not thy glory; may God protect you from all harm.

Anne   Why? When he that is now called my husband came to me, I wept my then-husband's corpse. When I looked into his face, I said to him: 'May you be cursed, for evicting me from the train of my life! And, when you marry, let sorrow haunt your bed; and may your wife – that poor blighted soul – be made to drink the misery I drank from your hand that placed the stone of death on my husband!' Before I could repeat this curse again, my woman's heart grossly grew captive to his honey words. Now my own soul's curse returns to my chest. He hates me and will be rid of me sooner not later.

Exit **Stanley** *and* **Anne**.

Elizabeth   Stay! Look back with me at the Tower. Oh, mute stones! Blind witnesses to our pain. I beg you give solace to my boys! Comfort the horror of their nights and the loneliness of their days, be gentle you inhuman womb. What have you left in me my pain, a mother's incinerated heart wailing at stones!

Scene Two, the palace

The coronation ceremony takes the form of an ancient war dance, 'Al Ardha' [10] *performed by males in chorus with swords and rifles.* **Richard** *stands in line with the dancers and performs the repetitive movements with them, raising and lowering swords and rifles in time with the drums and the chant. The child* **Prince Edward** *is downstage of the chorus, as if sleepwalking.* **Richard** *breaks from the chorus and removes the Iqal from the child's head and places it on his own, then uses the child's headscarf to blindfold his eyes. We are entering hallucinatory time.*

Richard   My cousin Buckingham!

Buckingham   My gracious Ruler?

Richard   Shall we wear these honours for a day; or shall they last, and we rejoice in them?

Buckingham   Forever may they last!

The Coronation Ceremony. Fayez Kazak, Faisal
Al-Ameeri. Photo by Ruud Jonkers.

Richard Buckingham, now I'll know if you are current gold
indeed! Young Edward lives: think now what I would say?

Buckingham Say on, my lord.

Richard I say I would be king.

Buckingham So you are.

Richard Am I king? It is so, but Edward lives.

Buckingham True, noble Prince.

Richard Bitter consequence, that Edward still should live:
'True, noble Prince!' You're so dull. Shall I be plain? I wish
the bastards dead! What do you say? Speak suddenly and be
brief.

Buckingham You may do as you please.

Richard You're all ice! Do I have your consent that they shall
die?

Buckingham I will resolve your grace immediately.

Buckingham *exits from the stage and enters his surveillance room, where* **Mr Richmond** *awaits him. They consult. The dance continues.*

Richard   Catesby!

Catesby   Order me!

Richard   Don't you know anyone whom corrupting gold would tempt unto a close exploit of death?

Catesby   I know a man whose humble means match not his haughty mind.

Richard   What is his name?

Catesby   Tyrrel.

Richard   I partly know the man. Go, call him hither. *(Exit Catesby.)* The deep revolving Buckingham no more shall be my counsellor – stops he now for breath? What news with you, Stanley?

Stanley   My cousin Dorset's fled to join with the foreigners.

Richard   Inform Anne to prepare my chamber, I will take a second wife! Why do you gape, moron?

Exit **Stanley**. *Enter* **Catesby**.

Catesby   I couldn't find Tyrrel.

Richard   Then?

Catesby   I will play his part.

Richard   Do you dare?

Catesby   Prove me.

Richard   Kill a friend of mine?

Catesby   I'd rather kill two enemies.

Richard   Quick-witted Catesby! Two deep enemies: I mean those bastards in the Tower.

Catesby   Let me have open means to come to them, and I'll rid you from the fear of them.

Richard   Say it is done, and I will prefer you.

Catesby   It's done, my Emir.

Enter **Buckingham**.

Buckingham   I have considered your late demand.

Richard   Dorset is fled to the foreigners.

Buckingham   I hear that news. I claim my due by promise. The oilfields of the North, which you promised, I should possess.

Richard   As I remember the late ruler did prophesy that foreign armies would rule this land!

Buckingham   Your promise.

Richard   Foreigners!

Buckingham   My Lord!

Richard   Do you not learn Arabic poetry, Buckingham?

Buckingham   Your promise of the oilfields.

Richard   'And teach him how to bow the arrow every day and when his arm was strong …' Finish the verse! Go on.

Buckingham   What?

Richard   'He shot me' – you bastard! Try another one, Counsellor: 'If you be not a hungry wolf, full of menace …' What's the end of that line, my advisor, remind me?

Buckingham   I don't follow.

Richard   'The foxes will piss on you!' Do you want to make me weep, Buckingham; why don't you learn poetry?

Buckingham   Do you keep your promise or no?

Richard   God protect me from my friends – as for mine enemies, I am apt enough.

Exit **Richard**.

Buckingham   Death for a man like me in a country like this carries no notes, no pertinent documents, no yea or nay votes. It's like the turnaround of a mildly soiled room in a well-run hotel. Turn, head, go find a door, walk through it.

Exit **Buckingham**.

Scene Three, the palace

Catesby *with blood on his hands and robes.*

Catesby   I swear I turned back twice. But He put out his hand. The Book was on the pillow. 'No!' I said, 'it's the Qur'an. It's haram. Can't do it. Haram.' Then one of them opened his eyes: a boy. Same age as my own. Can't do it. Can't. God, what did you make me of? Yesterday, I snapped my friend's neck and today these children. Filthy, dirty scab; rotten, useless chump! It wasn't me: it was the devil, the devil put out his hand.

(Sings.)
Damn you and damn all who begged for your love.
Damn all the lovers who seek only pain!
My crime in this life was to clear room for you in my heart
To love you is to slash open my veins.[11]

Scene Four, the palace

The women are assembled in mourning black. They are engaged in a Khammari dance.[12] *The words are spoken in the style of recitativo.*

Elizabeth   Ah, my young Princes!
Ah, my tender babies!
God slept when this was done and died when it happened.

Margaret   Now prosperity begins to mellow and drop into the rotten mouth of death.
Here in these confines slyly have I lurked, to watch the waning of mine adversaries.

Elizabeth   Oh blood-soaked earth!
Open your jaws, I will bury my live bones in you.

Margaret   Tell over your woes again by viewing mine.

Elizabeth   Fate's widow, triumph not in my woes.

Margaret   I told you then.

Elizabeth   Don't remind me.

Margaret   I called you then poor, painted Queen.

Margaret *beats* **Elizabeth** *with an Iqal.*

Where is your husband?
Your brothers?
Your children?
Gnash from the fat of your heart, gnash!
I am thirsty for revenge!

Elizabeth   God be my witness, I wept for your sorrows!

Margaret   Coo in your catastrophe, coo like an errant dove! You did usurp my place, and now you usurp the just proportion of my sorrow.

Elizabeth   Teach me how to curse and melt the human frame, teach me!

Margaret   Forbear to sleep the nights, and fast the days; compare dead happiness with living woe.

Elizabeth   My words are dull.

Margaret   Thy woes will make them sharp, and pierce like mine.

Scene Five, the military parade

Richard *is waving from a balcony at the passing military cavalcades. We hear the sound of military brass bands and crowds cheering.* **Elizabeth** *is brought to stand next to him.*

Elizabeth   Villain slave, where are my children?

King Richard   Sister, I must speak a word with you. You have a daughter with a fine mouth.

Elizabeth   Let her live and I'll corrupt her manners, stain her beauty.

King Richard   Wrong not her birth, she is of royal blood.

Elizabeth   To save her life, I'll say she is not.

King Richard   Know that from my soul I love thy daughter, and mean to make her queen of the Peninsula.

Elizabeth   Who do you mean shall be her King?

King Richard   Who else but the King in all his blood and guts.

Elizabeth   You?

King Richard   I.

Elizabeth   God save us!

King Richard   What say you, then, mother; you are best acquainted with her humour.

Elizabeth   Send her a pair of bleeding hearts; engrave her brothers' names on them, then watch how happily she weeps.

King Richard   What's done is dead. If fate did steal the kingdom from your sons, to make amends, I'll give it to your daughter. And in this we make a lie of destiny. Go then, my mother, to thy daughter; acquaint the princess with the sweet hours of marriage joy, the taste of man.

Elizabeth   What man? Her father's brother?

King Richard   Say that the King, which may command, entreats.

Elizabeth   That which the King's king forbids?

King Richard   She will be a high and mighty queen.

Elizabeth   To wail the tide, as her mother does.

King Richard   Your reasons are too shallow and too quick.

Elizabeth   They are too deep and dead as my infants in their grave.

King Richard   By my religion and my crown.

Elizabeth   You have profaned the first and usurped the second.

King Richard   I swear–

Elizabeth   Swear by something that you have not wronged.

King Richard   By the world.

Elizabeth   It's full of your foul wrongs.

King Richard   My father's soul.

Elizabeth   Your life dishonours it.

King Richard   By God.

Elizabeth   God's wrong is most of all. What can you swear by now?

King Richard   The time to come.

Elizabeth   Your past wrongs extend to your grave.

Richard *leaves the balcony and thrusts* **Elizabeth** *into a private space.*

King Richard   I swear you are an atheist!

Enter **Catesby** *with a branding iron.*

Elizabeth   Take me. I'll marry you, I'll give you children.

King Richard   What I seek runs in her veins.

Elizabeth   Shall I be tempted by the devil?

King Richard   If the devil tempt you to do good.

Elizabeth   You killed my children.

King Richard   But in your daughter's womb I bury them. Where in that nest of spicery they shall breed selves of themselves, to your recomforture.

Elizabeth   Shall I go win my daughter to thy will?

King Richard   And be a happy mother by the deed.

Elizabeth   You shall understand from me her mind.

Exit **Elizabeth**.

King Richard   A kiss of my true love.

The sound of the military band continues.

Scene Six, the war room

Richard   What news, Stanley?

Stanley   Western armies are on the seas.

Richard   Let them sink.

Stanley   Stirred up by Dorset, Buckingham and Morton they make for our lands, to claim your crown.

Richard   Is the chair empty? Is the sword unswayed? Is the King dead? The empire unpossessed? Why aren't you with them? Follow the foreign filth, sell your country?

Stanley   I never was, nor never will be false.

Richard   What did you name your son, Stanley?

Stanley   George Stanley.

Richard   Is that an Arabic name?

Ratcliffe   No, by God!

Stanley   What do you mean?

Richard   You are a traitor! Dispatch now and muster men and arms.

Stanley   Immediately.

Richard   Your son George Stanley remains as my guest. Be loyal to me or else his head falls like a head of corn.

Stanley   So deal with him as I prove true to you.

News Reader   Edward Courtney and his brother there are in arms in Dinevshire.

Richard   Devonshire!

News Reader   My liege, the Golfbags are in arms.

Richard   Guildfords!

News Reader   By the hour, more traitor rebels join them. The foreigners have sent infantry to Buckingham the traitor!

Richard   Only songs of death! Take that *(Slaps him.)* that you may bring me better news.

News Reader   It is so, my Lord.

Richard   Tell me, then!

News Reader   Sand storms have dispersed Buckingham's forces, he is lost and does not know where he wanders.

Richard   Has a bounty been announced for that traitor-dog, Buckingham?

Ratcliffe   It has.

Richard   Onwards, then, since Allah has sent nature's wrath and dispersed the invaders let us move on. If not to destroy the invaders, then to squash the heretic-kafirs inside this land!

Richard *places* **Ratcliffe** *and the News Reader on either side of him. He extends his hands and they sheepishly join hands with him. The three men charge off, screaming.*

Scene Seven, the palace

Dialogue is suppressed, furtive. In the distance we hear fighter jets and bombs falling. **Richard** *sits in* **Buckingham***'s surveillance booth, monitoring the conversation.*

Stanley   I have been sent to discuss with you preparations and protocol for your daughter's wedding to the King.

Elizabeth   The Night of Penetration.

Stanley   Yes.

Elizabeth   Excellent, my daughter is ready.

Stanley   When will the guests arrive?

Elizabeth   At 20:00 hours sharp on the agreed date.

Stanley   Which entrances?

Elizabeth   The Northern and Eastern Gates for those arriving by sea and private plane, well-wishers arriving on foot can use the Southern Gates.

Stanley   Staggered arrival?

Elizabeth   What on earth for? All together, my dear, I trust we have enough cutlery.

Stanley   You know I won't be able to attend.

Elizabeth   Why not?

Stanley   My son is guest of honour in the King's basement. It would be inappropriate of me to be seen at parties at a time like this.

Elizabeth   But you will uphold my daughter's honour, Stanley?

Stanley   With all I possess.

Elizabeth   To be free of the devil, we must give ourselves to the devil, Stanley.

Stanley   I know. May God ease our task.

Article Five

Scene One, York TV

Buckingham   Will not King Richard let me speak with him?

Catesby   Not until you've made your vile confession.

Buckingham   *(Reading a statement.)* I am Buckingham. I was the advisor to the palace. I am an agent of foreign imperial agencies. I spied on this country's most sensitive interests. And transmitted this information to my masters in order to weaken the state and engineer its downfall. I am a secret employee of the Mossad-CIA. I single-handedly orchestrated the death of the Crown Prince and his brother to weaken the position of the King. To all these things I confess and beg forgiveness from God and King Richard.

Catesby   May Allah bless him with long life!

Buckingham's confession. Raymond El Hosny and
Monadhil Daood. Photo by Ruud Jonkers.

They put a plastic bag on his head and asphyxiate him.

Scene Two, four images and a song

Ratcliffe *leads* **Anne** *across the stage. It is understood from the crossing that she is to be stoned to death.*
Catesby*, who will oversee the stoning, sings a love song:'Ya naas dallouni'.*
In the background, **Mr Richmond** *and an unidentified man are exchanging documents, maps, schedules.*
Elizabeth *looks through a pair of binoculars handed to her by Richmond.*

Scene Three, the battleground, a dreamscape

Catesby   *(Intoning a prayer.)* Forgive my deepest, blackest sins, my crimes, my soul this night is heavy, my life in your hands …

Ratcliffe *brings* **Catesby** *tea, then falls asleep.*

Richard   *(On the phone in* **Buckingham***'s surveillance suite.)*
Will the Ambassador not speak to me? I have a conscience that wants to talk to him about the consequences of being an enlightened man of learning! Where can I take this stray dog of mine? Where to kennel it? If my dog bites you, Ambassador, it will infect you and your frail masters – filth in: filth out! My hands are covered in it, but I don't boast otherwise you two-faced democrat dog! Now be careful what you say, Ambassador, you're in my country. Oh really? Well, I have snipers in The Hague too!

Enter **Margaret** *singing an old Syriac death song, pulling a horse. Behind her, the ghosts of* **Clarence***,* **Anne***,* **Hastings***,* **Rivers***,* **Grey***. Behind them,* **Mr Richmond***.*

Mr Richmond   *(Holding a Qur'an in his hand.)*
God and our good cause fight upon our side;
For what is he they follow? Truly, citizens,
A bloody tyrant and a homicide;
One that hath ever been God's enemy:
Then, if you fight against God's enemy,

God will in justice ward you as his soldiers;
I read it all right here in your Qur'an
Allah says: 'whoever defends himself
From being oppressed can not be blamed';
Chapter Forty Two, Verse Forty One
As-Shura, which means the Consultation
And that is what I'm saying to you all.
Then, in the name of God and all these rights,
Advance your standards, draw your willing arms.

Scene Four, the mounting of Al-Ummah

Richard   What can I say more than I have said? Who you face today are a gang of heretics, refugees from the face of justice and the ire of Allah! Foreigners, invaders, jailbirds and shantytown dwellers whose poverty has spewed them forth to die at your hands. They are envious-eyed with no honour in their souls. They saw you possessing oil and blessed with astonishing wives and they would restrain the one and disdain the other. And who leads them but a paltry heathen? A murtad[13] and a sproglet of Sykes-Picot. A grand conspirator who holds the Bible in one hand and buries the Torah in his heart, who wishes to turn you into a nation of castrati. If we be conquered, let men conquer us, not these bastard heathens who hold life dear and swill in its iniquities and vice as animals, exactly as animals! Down with the enmity of the enemy! May the losers lose![14] *(To* **Catesby***.)* Will Stanley bring his men?

Catesby   No.

Richard   Off with his son's head!

Catesby   The enemy is at the gates; we don't have time.

Richard   What's this horse called?

Catesby   Al-Ummah.[15]

Richard   Al-Ummah! Let me ride Al-Ummah! *(He unsheathes his sword.)* This, my Qadisiya![16] This, my Battle of Thiqar![17] On them! Victory sits on our helms.

Richard: A horse! A horse! My kingdom for a horse!
Fayez Kazak. Photo by Jonathan Player.

Margaret *turns the horse, rotating it furiously like a mechanical bronco in a Las Vegas bar.*

Richard   A horse! A horse! My kingdom for a horse!

The sound of two clean sniper shots, then silence.

Scene Five, the aftermath. Waves

Enter **Stanley***,* **Elizabeth***, then* **Mr Richmond***.* **Elizabeth**
translates between **Stanley** *and* **Mr Richmond***.*

Mr Richmond   God and your arms be praised, victorious friends,
The day is ours, the bloody dog is dead.
Ask him about his son – he alive?

Stanley   He is, my lord.

Mr Richmond   Good man! What men of name are slain on
either side?

Stanley   Many, many. *(***Stanley*** reads from a scroll.)*
Hamza Bin Abd Al Mutalib
Abu Thar Al Ghufarri
Summayah bint Khayyatt
Al Husein Bin Ali
Al Hassan Al Basri.

Mr Richmond   Inter their bodies as becomes their births:
Proclaim a pardon to the soldiers fled
That, in submission, will return to us:
What traitor hears me, and says not Amen?

Stanley*'s list of martyrs and* **Mr Richmond***'s speech, run
simultaneously.*

Stanley:	**Mr Richmond:**
Wafaa Al Amer	This land hath long been mad, and scarr'd herself;
Shafiq Al Athem	The brother blindly shed the brother's blood,
Mahdi Ben Barakah	
Muhammad Abdu	The father rashly slaughter'd his own son,
Abdullah Ibn Al Muqaffah	The son, compell'd, been butcher to the sire:
Omar Al Mukhtar	
Faraj Foudah	Alright, now: into Elizabeth's hands
Hussain Mroue	I place the reins of interim governance As mild precursor to free elections

Kamal Naser	Peace, prosperity and smiling plenty:
Sami Taha	Abate the edge of traitors, yes please God,
Ahmed Orabi	Save us from the scourge of insurgency
Khalil Hawi	
Samir Qaseer Abdulrahman Al Kawakebi	That would splint the broken arm of terror, And make this dry land weep in streams of blood!
Mohammad Mossadegh	God say amen! Terror God Amen.
Yusuf Al Athamah	Terror God Amen.

Beneath these words, a Jihadi song builds in the background until it is intolerably loud.

A figure with masked face   *(Loading and firing a rocket-propelled grenade.)* Allah-U-Akbar!

End

Notes

1 It is important that this actor speaks a *different language* to the others.
2 Akhwan– an Islamic religious militia which formed the main military force of the Arab ruler Ibn Saud.
3 Snafi– a medication for erectile dysfunction.
4 Qur'anic exhortations.
5 Iqal: a tightly woven black woollen head strap, worn by males in the Arabian Gulf.
6 Qur'an: Al Maidah, verse 32 (5:32).
7 Qur'an: Al 'Isra', verse 33 (17:33).
8 Abul Qassim Al-Shabi, Tunisian poet.
9 Act Four is supremely ritualistic in which the threads of linear, causal time and cyclical, ahistorical time are interwoven and meshed. This contrast in temporality is accentuated by the alternating female–male structure of the scenes. To render these ideas tangible, the act is approached essentially through music that draws on the traditions of song, ceremonial dance and witchcraft in the Arabian Gulf to create a swelling, cascading, hallucinatory series of musical and visual tableaux.
10 Al Ardha: a war dance performed predominantly by tribes in the Najd region of the Arabian peninsula. The dance is thought to have pre-Islamic origins; consisting of a chorus of dancers and singers and lines of percussion players, its contemporary use is restricted primarily to celebrations and festivals.
11 An Iraqi folk song.
12 Khammari dance, traditional dance for one female dancer, practised in the northern Gulf region, Kuwait.
13 Murtad: rejecter of the Islamic faith.
14 The expression is Qur'anic, but notorious for its use by the late Iraqi tyrant Saddam Hussein in his speech marking the eleventh anniversary of the end of the Iran–Iraq war, 1999.
15 Al-Ummah, Arabic for the Nation of Believers.
16 Qadisiya, decisive engagement between the Arab Muslim armies and the Sassanid Persian army which gave the Arab Muslims the conquest of Persia.
17 Thiqar, a pre-Islamic battle between Arab tribesmen and a Sassanid Persian army.

The Speaker's Progress:
A play in the shadow of revolution

Conceived by: Georgina Van Welie and Sulayman Al Bassam
Written by: Sulayman Al Bassam
(October 2010–September 2011)

Note on the text and language: The ostensible aim of the performance, as described by the Speaker at the outset, is to make a 'scientific reconstruction' of a play from a previous era.[1] The elements of the reconstructed text are shown in italics. In terms of the languages of the play, it's important to note that a central conceit of the performance hinges on the fact that the Speaker addresses the audience in their language – the language of the receiving venue – whereas the other envoys speak to one another and undertake the reconstruction in their own, distinct, language. This becomes critical in the gulling of the Mullah scene, where the Mullah is duped into making utterances in a language he is completely unfamiliar with. In the case of the original production, the envoys spoke in Arabic and the Speaker addressed the audience in English. A director working in one language needs to decide how to deal with this play of languages. To provide the English reader with a sense of this, the Arabic is in regular font and the English – used principally in direct address to the audience – is in bold.

The setting:[2] The events are set in the theatre where the play is being performed. At the start, the stage is arranged as if for a lecture. In the foreground, a large projection screen. On the lip of the stage a video camera stands on a short tripod. On stage left a speaker's podium, equipped with light, microphone and national flag. On stage right a sound technician's table with lamp, reels of tape, an old reel-to-reel recorder, a bell and other items. Behind the front projection screen is a spartan space that resembles a criminal forensic laboratory. At the centre of the laboratory is a rectangular section of raised wooden stage, divided with chalk into numbered squares. On either side of the raised platform are steel laboratory tables cluttered with stage props and costume accessories in evidence bags, monitoring equipment, plans and archive images from the 1963 performance. Next to the sound technician's table is a sound and time monitoring point from which the envoys take it in turns to listen to the original recording on headsets and mouth the lines to their colleagues, ensuring the reconstruction is played out in synchronicity with the archive material. At the rear of the wooden platform is a second projection screen onto which photographic evidence, stills from the 1963 performance and scanned copies of the director's notebooks are projected.

Note to the actors: The challenge of this text lies in the actors mastering dynamic levels of characterization. The actors need to play and escalate multiple levels of character: non-actors/envoys; characters in the inset play; individuals faced with turmoil and great uncertainty. Apart from *The Former Actress* and *The Speaker*, who have previous professional theatre experience, the remaining envoys need to assume their roles as amateur performers. It's important this is done without inviting parody. Amateur actors in performance are generally quite nervous, focused and extremely serious. They are neither po-faced mummers, nor comic buffoons. Capturing this earnestness and excitement will help clarify the stakes at the beginning of the play. The envoys are on a state mission. They have been sent by a totalitarian regime. They are being closely observed by the state video camera at the front of the stage and co-monitored by their fellow envoys. There is no room for error, or for making light of the task at hand. Clandestine bonds of trust and complicity can be assumed to exist between some of the envoys, but this back-story is only of value in so far as it is brought out in the performance. Within the logic of the mission, the reconstruction of the historical play and the exposure of its ideological impurity is the supreme aim. Improvisation, inaccuracy, accident, coincidence and humour are all antithetical to this mission. The performance functions best when the underlying tension between its rational, totalitarian aim and the human inconsistency of its methods is crystallized. In approaching the characters of the inset play, the envoys need to adopt an attitude of distrust. They are representing enemies of the state. Gestures, impersonation, embodiment of character, complicity with the live audience are all dangerous tools in so far as they expose the envoy to unwanted scrutiny. Use of these tools should, therefore, be carefully staggered and gradually rise, as it were, with the heat of performance. As the performance develops and the public personas of the envoys are exposed to increasing duress, the actors cannot rely entirely on guidance from the characters in the inset play – this would flatten their evolution of character and make their 'improvisations' (in which they challenge and deviate from the reconstructed text) meaningless. Their journey is not from faceless citizen of a totalitarian state into a character from *Twelfth*

Night; rather, it is a spontaneous individual and collective journey from oppression into freedom. In this, the actors will need to draw on their character as performers, their own individuality as actors and their contagious relationship both with one another on stage and with the presence of the obscure partner – the audience. The Sound Technician who accompanies the performance follows a similar development, moving from the utilitarian function in service of the reconstruction into a source of improvised and dynamic music.

The rhythm in performance demands an efficient functionality from the envoys and confident accompaniment from the Speaker. To create the right dynamic of contrast with the moments of danger and chaos, the laboratory needs to be established as a well-oiled machine, which carries its own inexorable momentum.

The Envoys:
Speaker
Representative of the Writers' Union
Representative of the National Tourist Board
Representative of the Council of Virtue
Representative of the Women's League
Representative of the Student Union
Former Actress
Young Woman
An Actress from the Golden Era
A sound technician, later a Musician

Characters in the Reconstructed play[3]
The Ruler – *a man in love – performed by the Representative of the Council of Virtue*
Thuraya – *a woman in search of freedom – performed by the Representative of the Women's League*
Nishami – *her housemaid – performed by the Young Woman*
Tagtiga – *her drunken uncle – performed by the Representative of the Writers' Union*
Faris – *his rich friend – performed by the Representative of the National Student Union*
Mullah Farhan – *a reactionary – performed by the Representative of the Council of Virtue*
Feylooti – *a blind fool – performed by the Representative of the Council of Virtue*
Fawz – *a female outsider – performed by the Former Actress*
A Sea Captain; Courtiers – *seen on the archive footage only*

Act One, the Discourses

Scene One

As the audience enters the theatre, archive film is projected onto the projection screen, showing the audience awaiting the start of the performance in 1963. Enter Sound Technician. He prepares reels, puts on his headphones, nods to the Speaker, who enters with a folder and stands at the podium.

Speaker *(In Arabic.)* Peace be upon you, good evening and welcome. In light of the relations that link our two sovereign nations in friendship and trust and out of respect for our hosts, I will be addressing tonight's lecture in your language.

(In the language of the host venue.) **Good evening and welcome. As some of you may know I used to be a theatre maker. But, for several years now – since the closures – I, and others like me, have been in forced retirement. Theatres and other public venues have been closed. The act of performance itself has been criminalized as part of a series of pre-emptive measures including the establishment of emergency law, nocturnal curfews, military courts and the suspension of the internet to guard against the undermining of national unity and halt the spread of the mental plague and associated civil unrest that has gripped so much of our region in recent times.**

Let me be definitive: I support these actions. Indeed, during the Artists' Trials, I made my position clear by giving a detailed public denouncement of all of my previous work. I even offered to set fire to a theatre.

I would happily be in my country now, defending our right to self-definition, but we have been terribly wronged and viciously misunderstood; therefore, to address these misconceptions our leaders have seen it fit for us to be here, with you, tonight. Though we no longer have need of theatre as a form of enquiry or representation, we understand your attachment to this outdated medium and will therefore meet you halfway, as it were, embodying our discourse in

a language that you will recognize and understand, whilst respecting the regulations that now govern our cultural expression.

Before we go any further, allow me to take you back in time to a period when revolution and, for that matter, theatre were all the rage. This is not the first time our region has witnessed the tumult of revolution: 50 years ago, it was swimming in it.

On the projection screen, book covers from the early 1960s are displayed: A Guide to Arab Revolution; The Arab Revolution.

Alongside tracts like these, were plays that tried in their own way to stir up trouble in our stable lands.

Here, *(Displaying the archive tapes.)* are the reels of one such performance, extracts from which will serve as an example of past mistakes, and proof of the corruptive, insidious and illusory nature of false freedom. Lights down: we'll begin.

The archive recording plays on the projection screen. We see the stage curtain opening to reveal the Ruler and his court, with musicians. Here follows the text of the archive recording:

Ruler   *(Addressing the musicians.) Do you know what love does to a man's breathing? To his lungs, to his eyes, to his dreams! You do not! You play false and your eyes wander. I think I'll fold you all into a fish trap and give you a straw to breathe from.*

Servant   *Shall we prepare the fish trap, Shaikh?*

Ruler   *What trap, what fish? When I am the one ensnared and bound, clawed and mauled, when my soul is hanging like ripped meat from the beak of a predator named Thuraya! Music is the food of love and love is the blood of freedom and freedom is the mother of progress (The audience erupts in spontaneous applause.) and she this woman, Thuraya, is the heart of progress. (Addressing the Minister.) Cousin, you will announce a prize for the greatest love song of all time. The winner will receive the equivalent of 40 days' worth of this country's oil wealth; one for each day of Thuraya's mourning.*

Minister   *That's 10 per cent of the national income!*

Ruler   *Not from the state coffers, you criminal – from my own wealth.*

Minister   *But, cousin–*

Ruler   *Scatter my messengers, burn my palaces, but never can you extinguish the flames in this heart! I want to churn the sea with songs, the desert to turn green with shades of love poetry, the trees to fill with migrant birds who nest to learn new melodies. The prize will carry her name. It will be called: Thuraya! Cousin Mutlag, I'll be listening for the announcement on the state broadcast after Isha prayers.*

(Recording burns out.)

Speaker   Here, the scene burns out. Small, iconic scenes like this have become a source of obsession for many misguided segments of our society. Cited, quoted, uploaded and disseminated, this recording has generated a potent and dangerous mixture of nostalgia and civil disobedience. Our Leaders have spoken at length of their condemnation of these romantic tendencies and the scent of foreign intervention has already been sniffed.

Tonight, through a precise and scientific reconstruction of this decadent play, we reclaim our own history, provide a definitive guide to the confused and through you, dear friends, convey a message to the world at large that will defuse mounting hysteria and expose once and for all the hollowness of these derivative forms of cultural expression and their absolute *antithesis to progress*.

What you are about to see in no way aspires to be described as theatre and functions in full accordance with the laws of our land. Any member of the audience attracted here for what they might have heard about our previous works, namely, a salacious exposé of life under dictatorship, is welcome to leave now. Best wishes, full refund.

Envoys!

Enter the envoys, wearing lab coats, latex gloves, carrying scripts, clipboards and scientific objects. The Representative of the National Tourist Board carries a metre rule. The envoys line up in front of the projection screen.

To repeat: we have no desire to embody the decadence. The individuals before you are not actors: they are envoys.

The Representative of the National Tourist Board uses the metre rule to ensure he is at the correct distance from the nearest female envoy.

We respect the traditional law that proscribes a minimum of 90 centimetres between males and females. We are as ideologically neutral as palaeontologists armed with little more than tongs, a brush, a magnifying glass and a metre. *(Addressing the envoys, in Arabic.)* **Introduce yourselves.**

Rep. Council of Virtue   My name is Faisal – no need to mention the family name, right?

Speaker   Not applying for asylum, are we?

Rep. Council of Virtue   No! I'm an envoy from the Council of Virtue.

Speaker   You're not, in any way, an actor?

Rep. Council of Virtue   God forbid.

Speaker   *(Introducing the Sound Technician.)* We also have with us an international sound specialist, Mr Lewis, expert in all manner of reconstruction of decadence.

Rep. Women's League   Carole – envoy from the Women's League.

Former Actress   Amal, a former actress.

Young Woman   *(Shies away from microphone.)*

Speaker   Young and confused, move on.

Rep. Tourist Board   Fayiz, envoy from the National Tourist Board – formerly a car mechanic.

Rep. Student Union   Nassar, envoy from the Democratic League of Students.

Rep. Writers' Union   Nicolas, envoy from the Writers' Union.

Speaker **Writers, artists, women's rights, tourism and free students, which proves, if ever proof were needed, how misunderstood we are.** *(An actress from the Golden Era appears via video link on the projection screen.)* **We have joining us now, via satellite, an important witness to the events we are reconstructing.** *(In Arabic.)* **Introduce yourself, please.**

Actress from Golden Era Hanan Hajj Ali, former actor.

Speaker You were involved in the original performance we are reconstructing tonight, in 1963?

Actress from Golden Era I was. The theatre has always been a temple of truth.

Speaker In the age of falsehood, perhaps. What was it to be an actor in those days?

Actress from Golden Era It was to be one who digs the dykes around the city,
Tempers the winds and tides of oblivion,
A lighthouse in the fog,
A witness to the crime,
The memory of a mother's song,
A firework glinting in the curve of a child's eye!

Speaker And now?

Actress from Golden Era Now? The theatres are closed. Music, like masturbation, is a secret habit; women are the guardians of tribal values, show me a mouth that's not been filled with gold or silenced with sand … Let's leave it to God.

Speaker *(Cutting her short.)* **Thank you! We are grateful to Madam Hanan, who has provided us with the original performance script from the 1963 play.** *(Envoys hold up their scripts.)* **And also the director's book from the original performance.** *(Envoys display clipboards.)*

Rep. Tourist Board *(The Representative of the Tourist Board indicates the video camera.)*

Speaker   Yes, the Ministry of Information is making a recording of this evening's events, strictly for archive purposes. Our second article of evidence, the sea coast after a shipwreck!

Scene Two

On the archive film we see a woman, Fawz, and a Sea Captain stood before a painted coastal backdrop.

Fawz   *Where are we?*

Sea Captain   *This is Ilyaal.*

Fawz   *Who rules here?*

Sea Captain   *A noble Shaikh in nature as in name.*

The archive recording freezes, leaving Fawz's face on screen.

Speaker   Here, the sound is interrupted. Therefore, in the pursuit of our declared objectives, we have set about to reconstruct this lost performance using parts of the sound reel that remain intact and the fragments that reappear from time to time on the reel. *(The projection screen is raised to reveal the laboratory.)* **The laboratory: a blessed bower. Through these simple instruments we achieve near total correspondence with the original artefact, without the pain of imitation. Here we make music that does not perturb the air – ha!**

The Former Actress and the Representative of the Student Union take up their positions on the raised platform in preparation for the reconstruction of the scene.

Speaker   Introduce your characters.

Former Actress   Fawz.

Rep. Student Union   The Sea Captain.

Speaker   We pick up from where the sound cut out, 'Who rules here? / A noble ruler in nature as in name.'

A bell rings to indicate the beginning of the reconstruction of this scene. Envoys follow the text and stage directions from their

clipboards, while other Envoys monitor them, intermittently
correcting their positions and gestures.

Fawz *I have heard of him from my father – he is a good ruler!*

Sea Captain: *But he suffers terribly from the pangs of love.*

Envoy   Move to B4.

Fawz *A ruler suffering from love?*

Sea Captain *He loves so much, announced a prize for the finest*
love song that will bring untold riches to the singer.

Envoy   Turn your head 70 degrees.

Fawz *And who is the woman who turns rulers into lovers?*

Sea Captain *Thuraya!*

Envoy   Eyes dilate, mouth opens: amazement!

The Former Actress enacts amazement.

Sea Captain *The daughter of a rich merchant. First her mother*
died, then her father died, then her brother died and she not even
married, all tangled in the weeds of mourning.

Fawz *I want to meet her.*

Sea Captain *She'll see no one. Not even the Shaikh's*
messengers.

Fawz *But I'm–*

Envoy   D3. *(Both envoys move to D3, so the instruction is*
corrected.) Male to D3!

Sea Captain *Follow me.*

Fawz *Where?*

Sea Captain *To the police! Telegram your kin, tell them you're*
alive.

Envoy   Enact the desire to disappear!

The Former Actress is taken aback by this instruction and hesitates.

Envoy   *(From the sound monitoring post, cueing the Former Actress.) I beg you, and I'll pay you,*

Conceal me what I am, and be my aid ...

Through her hesitation, the Former Actress falls out of sync with the sound recording. The envoy monitoring the sound recording indicates there is an error in the reconstruction. The Sound Technician presses his buzzer to stop proceedings.

Speaker   *(To the audience.)* **Our apologies. You appreciate the duress imitating acts antithetical to virtue puts us under. Take it back.**

The Sound Technician rewinds the reel-to-reel machine, the envoys reassume previous positions.

Envoy   Female in A3, Male in C2.

The Sound Technician presses the buzzer to resume proceedings.

Fawz   I beg you, and I'll pay you,
Conceal me what I am, and be my aid.
I'll serve this Shaikh,
Thou shalt present me to him as an eunuch;
It will be worth your trouble, for I can sing
And speak to him in many sorts of music,
That will allow me very worth his service.

Sea Captain   Be you his eunuch and I'll your mute be.

Bell signals the end of the reconstructed scene.

Former Actress   Here, she puts on the captain's jacket and transforms herself into a member of the opposite sex.

Speaker   *(To the audience.)* **A magnifying glass is not a mirror. This is a reconstruction of a historical performance and we do not in any way seek to make a new performance, challenge, question or reflect our reality through–**

Rep. Tourist Board   Excuse me.

Speaker   What is it?

Rep. Tourist Board   She's dressing up as a man.

Speaker   Yes, it's–

Rep. Tourist Board   This was not shown to the committee.

Speaker   Plenty wasn't shown to the committee – there was no time.

Rep. Tourist Board   I have the minutes of the committee hearing.

Speaker   I have a licence.

Rep. Tourist Board   I'll see it.

Speaker   **Ladies and Gentlemen, our dear colleague from the National Tourist Board is inquiring about the commission by which we perform for you tonight.** *(To the Representative of the Tourist Board.)* Stamp: Ministry of Information. Stamp: Ministry of Foreign Affairs. All's in order.

The Representative of the National Tourist Board takes the paper from the Speaker and shows it to the surveillance camera. The Representative of the Writers' Union takes advantage of this altercation to begin uncorking a bottle of wine.

Rep. Tourist Board   May I clarify one thing?

Speaker   Surely.

Rep. Tourist Board   The National Tourist Board does not regard a woman dressing up as a man as part of our country's tourist attractions. It is not on the list.

The wine cork pops noisily out of the bottle. The Representative of the Tourist Board turns in alarm. The Sound Technician promptly sounds the bell for the reconstruction to recommence. The Former Actress and the Representative of the Council of Virtue swiftly take up their positions on the raised platform.

Rep. Council of Virtue   *(Introducing his character.)* The Ruler.

On the projection screen we see a carnet de mise-en-scène, *showing colour-coded stage trajectories and cue lines.*

Speaker   *(Holding the* carnet de mise-en-scène.*)* Refer yourself to the drawings.

On the raised platform, Fawz is now dressed as a male servant.

Ruler   *Fawz?*

Fawz   *Command me, my King!*

Ruler   *How long have I known you?*

Fawz   *Three days, you of the long life.*

Ruler   *Whether it's the honesty I sense in your soul or the skill of your tongue, whatever it is I have opened my heart to you like a woman.*

Fawz   *Your praise embarrasses me.*

The Speaker signals his dissatisfaction to the Sound Technician, who presses the buzzer to stop the reconstruction.

Speaker   Faisal, please. You are playing the Ruler; show some dignity, some charisma!

Rep. Council of Virtue   I'm not here to act.

Rep. Tourist Board   Well said, boy!

Speaker   The laboratory protects you. Try harder: a Ruler!

The bell restarts the reconstruction.

Ruler   *I need you to undertake a mission. How's your falconry?*

Fawz   *I have a good hand, my bird soars high and dives hard as stones.*

Ruler   *I need you to be that bird diving unseen.*

Fawz   *Your prey?*

Ruler   *More precious than my own eyes: Thuraya.*

Fawz   *She's no bustard, my Lord, and craftier than a magpie.*

Ruler   *Fear not: you have what other men lack–*

Fawz   *I rather lack what they have–*

The Representative of the Writers' Union chuckles at the innuendo and is swiftly upbraided by a glance from the Representative of the Tourist Board.

Ruler   *You will carry the sentence and text of my love.*

Fawz   *O heavy sentence! What if she won't let me in?*

The Speaker removes his suit jacket and signals to the Representative of the Student Union to place it on the Representative of the Council of Virtue's shoulders – an improvised costume element to help him overcome his timidity, which he does.

Ruler   *Lay siege to her house. Deliver the text unblemished, unperverted, entire. You will have tents, food, gifts, men – even a generator!*

Fawz   *But I'm too young!*

Ruler   *Your youth will make her muscles tense, your poems make her tremble; when she trembles, slip in my name, just like that, slip it in. Bring me her heart and I swear you will live like a King.*

Fawz   *I'll speak of love as only lovers can, I know the sleepless night and the breathless day and I'll make her endure them.*

Ruler   *She's dry as a desert.*

Fawz   *If there's moisture in her, I'll feel it.*

A group of envoys laugh boisterously at the innuendo. In response, the Representative of the Tourist Board taps the metre rule emphatically on the steel laboratory table.

Speaker   *We despise filth!*

Ruler   *If you touch her, I'll blacken your face with tar!*

Fawz   *My metaphor undid me–*

Ruler   *Go. I entrust my love to you, like Solomon to the hoopoe.*
Give me your hand.

Bell signals the end of the reconstructed scene. The Speaker steps
onto the raised wooden platform, ostensibly to reclaim his jacket
from the Representative of the Council of Virtue.

Speaker   *(To the audience.)* **We know this character is a**
woman, masquerading as a man. The Ruler does not know
this. We know more than the Ruler. *(The Speaker surreptitiously*
places a small, red notebook into the pocket of the Former
Actress's lab coat.) **What you call dramatic irony, we regard as**
the toxic seedlings of an anti-social process.

Rep. Writers' Union   I've written a poem about that.

Speaker   It's not part of the reconstruction–

Rep. Writers' Union   But it was awarded a state prize.

Speaker   A state prize! We'll have to hear it.

Rep. Writers' Union   *(Addressing the Representative of the*
Tourist Board, who listens with suspicion at first, then glowing
pride.) If I knew more than you, my King of Kings:
Then summers, winters, all my springs
Are dead, dry, waterless things,
And in submission to your rod
Like Abraham to almighty God,
Dumb with joy, I'd load the gun
And empty it in my own son
I'd blow his brains and, in good turn,
Undo the father of the sperm.

Your looks, your eyes, your manly gaze
Where to start or end our praise
Your mother's breast, your father's loins,
The brow that shines from all our coins?
O, never say your line ends here
Or birth in us a cruel despair
Take women, virgins – don't be mild –
Bestow on us your chosen child

That as you mount us, so your sons
May one day serve their citizens.

Though faults you have, your virtues thin
To us you're pure as heroin;
A poppy bulb, your iron fist
An ornate pipe your long, black list;
Into the void, it sucks the name
Of every dark, crystal shame
To feed the endless, hungry flame.

Wrap your hands around my throat,
Of honour there's no finer coat
Squeeze tighter, prone the gorge to pay
Right tribute to its dying day
And loud, I cry, with dying breath:
Come now, o sweet and happy death!

All clap.

Speaker   **Uplifting poetry! Unlike the next excerpt of decadence we are obliged to present.**

Scene Three

Speaker   **This scene takes place in the house of Thuraya, the same Thuraya that the Ruler wishes to woo. It is a house draped in the cloak of mourning, but the sombre tones of the Quran are quickly uprooted by the nauseous excesses of the Drunken Uncle–**

Rep. Writers' Union   Sono io!

Speaker   **He speaks some Italian.** *(Continuing his narration.)* **… and his entourage – Nishami, the house maid; Faris, the Rich Idiot; and Feylooti, a blind fool.**

To identify the characters they are playing, the envoys obediently raise their hands on cue.

Speaker   **For the purposes of our demonstration and to allow you to apprehend the gravity of this innocent-seeming**

sub-plot, we have digitally suppressed the sound of the dialogue leaving only the sounds of the audience reaction, which clearly expose the corrupting intentions of the scene, without you being distracted by the quality of the acting, which is irrelevant.

We hear the sound of the audience from the 1963 production. On the archive film, we see Tagtiga and Nishami seated on a bench in Thuraya's courtyard. Between them is an old radio transistor tuned into a melodious reading from the Quran. Tagtiga is visibly annoyed by the sound of the Quran and extends his arm to turn the radio off. Nishami slaps his hand. This repeats several times to the boundless amusement, hoots and cackles of the 1963 audience. The envoys on the raised wooden platform read from their scripts to provide voiceover for the archive film. The sound of the Quran on the radio is provided by an envoy from a monitoring table.

Tagtiga reaches out his hand to turn off the radio.

Nishami   *(Slapping his hand.)* No.

Tagtiga *reaches out his hand to turn off the radio.*

Nishami   *(Slapping his hand.)* No, no, no!

Tagtiga   *(Emphatically turning the radio off.)* I swear we'll hear a love song!

The 1963 audience explodes into raucous laughter.

Speaker   From the Holy Quran to a love song: is this valid art? Next clip!

Nishami   *My lady Thuraya will go mad with your drunkenness and caterwauling!*

Tagtiga   *Will my niece never tire of mourning? Not even the Hussein had this much blubber and wailing. She's diseased and needs a doctor.*

Nishami   *She complained bitterly about you today.*

Tagtiga   *Who to?*

Nishami   *Mullah Farhan.*

On the archive film, we see Mullah Farhan poke his head through a window above the courtyard, listening to the conversation below, unseen. He is a stock character from Arab comedy at the time, an Islamist with a long beard, shortened thowb, armed with a whipping stick. The Representative of the Tourist Board, who will assume the role of the Mullah, steps onto the raised wooden platform, wearing a stage beard and waving the metre rule. He copies the Mullah's silent reactions.

Speaker   The Mullah, the only God-fearing, upright character in the scene–

Rep. Tourist Board   Present!

Tagtiga   Ah the rage! I the son of a nobleman forced to watch imposters lay siege to my own house!

Nishami   She cherishes his company above anyone else's.

Tagtiga   Because she's sick!

Nishami   Because you left her alone with him.

Tagtiga   I brought her Faris.

Nishami   The idiot Prince!

Tagtiga   A true prince!

Nishami   Who stinks of arak – a lecherous, bad poet, he is.

End of clip.

Speaker   Faris, the Rich Idiot, also loves Thuraya–

The Representative of the Tourist Board, sniffing out the source of the scent of alcohol, approaches the Representative of the Writers' Union. Fast, furtive, non-demonstrative dialogue.

Rep. Writers' Union   What?

Rep. Tourist Board   I can smell it.

Rep. Writers' Union   Keep your distance: 90 centimetres!

Rep. Tourist Board   The metre divides members of the opposite sex.

Rep. Writers' Union   I am of the opposite sex, I'm a hermaphrodite, how's that? Keep away!

Rep. Tourist Board   What's in that cup?

Rep. Writers' Union   Not much.

Rep. Tourist Board   Give me the cup!

Rep. Writers' Union   You want this cup? *(Downs the contents of his cup in one gulp and hands over the empty cup.)* Here's the cup!

The Representative of the Tourist Board smells the cup, returns to his monitoring station and carefully bags the object into a transparent evidence bag.

Speaker   *(To the audience.)* **Civil harmony is strained from the moment we begin to play with theatre. It contaminates. It sours. It poisons.**

The Representative of the Writers' Union makes an apologetic sign of deference to the Speaker. The other envoys, eager to resume the reconstruction on the raised wooden platform, have assumed their next positions.

Speaker   **Next clip.** *(The archive film resumes. In it, we see Faris enter the Courtyard with a bouquet of flowers, followed by Feylooti the Blind Fool.)* **Faris, the Rich Idiot, supplies the Drunken Uncle with the means required to maintain his lifestyle, and–**

The Representative of the Student Union, carrying the bouquet of flowers in line with the archive footage, has smuggled a second cup of wine onto the raised platform and surreptitiously hands it to the Representative of the Writers' Union who, with a self-satisfied grin, raises it to salute the health of the Representative Tourist Board.

Speaker   **And, in return, the Drunken Uncle strings the idiot along with the promise of Thuraya's hand.**

The Representative of the Women's League moves into the centre of the raised platform and holds her right hand aloft, as an item of evidence. It is gloved in white silk. With her wrist and fingers, she makes a distinct, balletic movement with her hand in the air: this choreographed hand movement is a sign that will be relayed to and imitated by other envoys. Hereinafter it is referred to as the 'revolutionary signal'.

Speaker *(Referring to the revolutionary signal.)* **The object of so many desires ... Faris, the Rich Idiot is a poet.**

Faris My heart has been split in two, like a melon that fell from a Daihatsu.

The archive film runs into a technical problem and repeats a series of frames endlessly. Obedient to the rules of the reconstruction, the envoys on the raised wooden platform repeat the same cycle of actions like giddy automatons. The Representative of the Women's League remains centre stage with her gloved hand raised; Faris the Rich Idiot raises and lowers the bouquet of flowers; Feylooti the Blind Fool wanders back and forth, Tagtiga raises and lowers his arm to applaud the poetry.

Speaker   And so it continues – endless cycles of debauchery and nostalgia. It lurks within us like a disease. We are harshest on ourselves and draw strength from our strife. Enough of this dirty little scene! *(Bell signals the end of the reconstructed scene.)* **Time for a musical interlude!**

On the screen we see the words 'Musical Interlude' as the Speaker and actors wait in total silence, without movement and count ten seconds.

Thank you.

Normal movement resumes.

Scene Four

The envoys move around the laboratory assuming their positions in preparation for the next phase of the reconstruction. On the raised platform, with minimal props, the Representatives of the

Tourist Board, the Women's League and the Young Woman. A black-and-white photograph, projected behind them, shows a still from the 1963 production. The scene is inside Thuraya's house.

Rep. Tourist Board   The Mullah reciting the Quran.

Rep. Women's League   Thuraya standing by the window.

Young Woman   Nishami holding the mirror.

The bell announces the start of a reconstruction.

Nishami   *Are you sick?*

Thuraya   *No.*

Nishami   *Drowsy?*

Thuraya   *No.*

Nishami   *He sent you flowers.*

Thuraya   *Which one?*

Nishami   *The one I said looked like a donkey and you said no, more bovine.*

Thuraya   *Oh, him.*

Nishami   *The Ambassador to Geneva. The one your uncle envies.*

Thuraya   *Mullah?*

Mullah   *Madam?*

Thuraya   *What say you?*

Mullah   *Ambassadors are oiled in deceit.*

Thuraya   *No, then.*

Nishami   *The Minister of Commerce sent you a gold watch.*

Thuraya   *He is very kind. Mullah?*

Mullah   *The Minister has peeled skin off the people's backs to place gold on your wrists.*

Thuraya   *(To Nishami) You keep it, dear. How I ache!*

Nishami   *Fever?*

Thuraya   *No.*

Nishami   *Where is the pain?*

Thuraya   *If only I knew!*

Envoy   Enter Feylooti.

Nishami   *Feylooti!*

Speaker   **In the interests of scientific accuracy, we have allowed ourselves to reconstruct ten-second clips of the lost music, in accordance with the Science of Sound Act.**

Feylooti sings an excerpt from a salacious folk song for ten seconds, the others count time on their fingers, at the end of ten seconds a buzzer sounds and Feylooti promptly desists.

Nishami   *Where have you been!*

Thuraya   *Five days you've left me alone.*

Feylooti   *I was at the poetry conference.*

The sound technician's table. Lewis Gibson. Photo by Rashid Al Bin Ali

Mullah   *Smells like it.*

Feylooti   *These are the flowers of paradise, Mullah, the flowers of paradise are not haram.*

Mullah   *If we were not in such genteel company, I would teach you a lesson or two.*

Feylooti   *How exciting! What would you do?*

Mullah   *My lady, do not encourage him with laughter – there's a quick remedy for his folly; canes with salted tips–*

Feylooti   *I beg you give the travesty his cane!*

Mullah   *May I eject this animal?*

Feylooti   *This is the prelude to dictatorship, mark my words.*

Thuraya   *You speak of politics.*

Mullah   *Can a drunkard poet speak of politics, my lady?*

Thuraya   *You speak of politics and I say there is nothing that I lack to speak of politics as well as any man.*

Feylooti   *Except a husband. I see you've pricked up your ears. Mullah!*

Thuraya   *I want to enter into politics.*

Envoy   The two females advance.

Mullah   *My lady, please–*

Thuraya   *Why not?*

Envoy   The two females advance.

Mullah   *It's not in your interests to think like that.*

Thuraya   *To speak of politics as well as any man, I lack for nothing.*

Feylooti   *(Imitating the Mullah.) Except a husband. I see your ears have pricked up, Mullah!*

Mullah   *Can I throw this animal out?*

Envoy   Enter Tagtiga. Drunk.

Tagtiga   *By God, someone's come back from Basra smelling ripe!*
(To Mullah.) Or is it you, goat herder?

Thuraya   *What is it to be drunk at ten in the morning, Uncle?*

Tagtiga   *Do not cast blame it excites my blood*
Cure me rather with another drop of grog.[4]
There's a boy leading an army outside.

Thuraya   *What kind of boy?*

Tagtiga   *A boy-like boy!*

Thuraya   *Mullah, go to them, if they're from the Shaikh, make it*
clear I will not see any more of his envoys.

Envoy   Exit Mullah and Nishami.

Tagtiga   *When the Ruler sends envoys to your door, you can't*
keep it shut for long.

Thuraya   *You are not to interfere with my personal life, Uncle.*

Tagtiga   *Stubborn wench! Come on, Feylooti, tell me about the*
real boys in Basra.

The Representative of the Council of Virtue sings a drinking song.

Speaker   *(Stopping the song after ten seconds.)* Enough!

Envoy   Enter Mullah and Nishami.

Mullah   *This boy has the devil in his eye; do not see him.*

Thuraya   *Did you send him packing?*

Mullah   *He's determined and has started setting up tents. He's*
got fiddlers with him; they're tuning up.

Envoy   Suggest desire.

The Young Woman places the fingertip of her latex glove between
her teeth and stretches it erotically. The Representative of the
Women's League emits a diminutive, erotic sob. Actions are
performed punctually and, once completed, neutrality is resumed.

Thuraya   *Let him in.*

Mullah   *But, madam, I–*

Thuraya   *I said let him in. Nishami, our veils! (The two women veil themselves.)*

Former Actress   *(Stepping onto the raised platform.)* Enter Fawz!

Fawz   *The honourable the lady of the house, which is she?*

Nishami   *We are both honourable ladies in this house.*

Thuraya   *This house is full of ladies!*

Fawz   *I demand to know which of you is Thuraya? (Gesturing to them to leave.)* Exit Mullah, exit Nishami. Go on!

The Representative of the Tourist Board and Young Woman step off the raised platform.

Thuraya   *Where lies your text?*

Fawz   *In the Ruler's bosom.*

Thuraya   *O, I have read it – it is heresy.*

Fawz   *Good madam, let me see your face.*

Thuraya   *Have you any commission from your lord to negotiate with my face? But we will draw the curtain and show you the picture. Is it not well done?*

Fawz   *Lady, you are the cruellest she alive,*
If you will lead these graces to the grave,
And leave the world no copy.

Thuraya   *O, sir, I will not be so hard-hearted; it shall be inventoried, and labell'd to my will – as – item, two lips indifferent red; item, two grey eyes with lids to them; item, one neck, one chin, and so forth. Were you sent hither to praise me?*

Fawz   *I see you what you are – you are too proud.*
My lord and master loves you!

Thuraya   *I cannot love him. Tell him that.*

Fawz   *If I did love you in my master's flame,*
In your denial I would find no sense;
I would not understand it.

Thuraya   *What would you if you were you?*

Fawz   *If I were I?*

Thuraya   *If you were you.*

Fawz   *Make me a willow cabin at your gate,*
And call upon my soul within the house;
Write loyal cantons of contemned love
And sing them loud even in the dead of night ...

She looks to the Speaker and glances at the red notebook.

I'd turn myself into a fruit seller
And set my body aflame in the square
I'd scratch your initials on the school walls
Take a bullet to the chest and turn the gash
Into a spring millions flock to drink from
I'd chant your name through a year of Fridays
Thuraya, Thuraya, Thuraya:
Huriya, Huriya, Huriya[5]!!!

The bell is rung, the buzzer sounded, the table banged, the lab descends into turmoil. The Representative of the Tourist Board locks the Former Actress in a choking grip, a scrum forms on the centre of the stage obscuring the Former Actress both from the video surveillance camera and the audience.

Rep. Writers' Union   *(Laconically.)* As poetry, purely as poetry – it was better than average.

Speaker   *(From the podium.)* It has been noted.

Rep. Tourist Board   Noted? *(Confrontationally.)* Noted?!

Former Actress   I'd like to say in my defence that–

Speaker   There's no need. **Time for the Tourist Board Presentation!**

Generic elevator music plays. On the projection screen we see images from the National Tourist Board: a beach; a school building; a state hospital; a gazelle in a desert landscape. The Representative of the Tourist Board is handed a microphone.

Rep. Tourist Board   Our public beaches: not a dead fish anywhere.
Our schools unearth – I mean – *bury* fundamentalism.
Our hospitals render death banal.
Our Arab Spring: see how the gazelle leaps over flowers in bloom.

Former Actress   Allow me to clarify …

The Female Envoys   Allow her to clarify … *(All the females in unison.)* Our Guardian knows best.

All smile. End of elevator music.

Speaker   Excellent. We continue.

Resuming the reconstruction, colder now.

Envoy   A6 and B3.

Thuraya   *You might do much. What is your parentage?*

Fawz   *Above my fortunes, yet my state is well: I am a gentleman.*

Thuraya   *Get you to your lord. I cannot love him; let him send no more –*
Unless perchance you come to me again
To tell me how he takes it. Fare you well.

Fawz   *Farewell, fair cruelty.*

The Former Actress approaches the Representative of the Women's League and discreetly places the red notebook into her lab-coat pocket, then descends from the raised platform, singing. The buzzer cuts short her song after ten seconds and she presents herself in front of the steel table of the Representative of the Tourist Board, empties her pockets, is fingerprinted and signs a paper that is filed into a box.

The fingerprinting of the Former Actress.
Fayez Kazak and Amal Omran. Photo by Mike Ritter.

Thuraya *Even so quickly may one catch the plague? Mullah!*

Rep. Tourist Board *(Fingerprinting the Former Actress.)* I'm busy!

Speaker *(To the Young Woman.)* Step in for him.

The Young Woman recuperates the Mullah's beard and steps hesitantly onto the raised platform to assume the role of the Mullah. During this time, the Representative of the Women's League discreetly hands the red notebook to the Representative of the Writers' Union.

Mullah *Here, madam.*

Thuraya *Run after that boy. He left this image in my mind, not an image, a swirl of images, not a swirl, a horde of possibilities, a promise, a pearl. Tell him I'll none of it.*

She hands her a pearl, then grasps the Young Woman's jaw firmly in her hand and, with her other hand, pointedly displays the choreographed hand movement, the revolutionary signal.

Thuraya   *If the youth will come this way tomorrow, I'll give him reasons for it. Go, Mullah.*

Mullah   *Madam, I will.*

The Young Woman steps off the platform and returns the beard to the Representative of the Tourist Board.

Thuraya: *(To the Speaker.) After a power cut, blindness descends,*
But for eyes accustomed to darkness,
Colours lie in ambush – blind fool!

The Representative of the Council of Virtue steps onto the platform as Feylooti, the Blind Fool. The Representative of the Student Union moves a light fixture into place. Feylooti and Thuraya turn to walk upstage, hold out their arms towards one another without touching, until the shadow of their hands clasped together is seen on the projection screen. The Representative of the Tourist Board escorts the Former Actress behind the projection screen and, again in shadow, we see him fumigate her.

Act Two, the Elaborations

The Tyranny of the Text

Scene One

Speaker *(To the audience.)* **Indeed, the journeys towards liberty are comic. But you seem not to be attuned to the dangers inherent in this type of resistance. The woman's improvisation, in which you played no small role, the reckless mixing of her wayward imagination with your complicit silence, the energy that fed her, the energy of a faceless mob shrouded in darkness, incited her to lose her mind and led us to this dangerous juncture. What you call playfulness is to us social suicide. Though we had hoped not to have to resort to such populist methods, it is clear that to help you perceive the dangers of which we speak, I must bring to bear the full brunt of my commission tonight: Bring on the costumes!**

The costumes from the 1963 production descend on a rack from above. Over the next few scenes, each envoy will gradually wear more and more elements of costume. The Representative of the Council of Virtue calls out the items from a list.

Rep. Council of Virtue The Ruler: two items. Feylooti, the Blind Fool: two items. Thuraya: four items. Nishami, the Housemaid: three items. Tagtiga, the Drunken Uncle: two items. The Rich Idiot: two items. Fawz: no items. The Mullah:–

Rep. Tourist Board *(Entering already dressed as the Mullah.)* Ten items. All other items are strictly off bounds. It's my scene next, what are we waiting for?

Former Actress *(Already on the raised platform.)* You!

Rep. Tourist Board *Who has the pearl? (Snatching it from the Young Woman.)* The bell, the bell!

Envoy Female in B3 her back to male in A4; male leans – her arse protrudes; she turns, male leans – her breasts protrude; she leaps.

Mullah   *Tricks, toys and trinkets: heresies all in the fires of hell!*

Envoy   Throws the pearl at her.

The Representative of the Tourist Board throws the pearl at the Former Actress.

Fawz   *How dare you throw stones at me, Mullah!*

Mullah   *You kneel and collect it, boy, you know it is a pearl, take it back to your master, let him cash it in elsewhere; Madam Thuraya will have none of your pirouettes and double chat.*

Fawz   *What pirouettes? What double–*

Mullah   *Your poetry and devilry – do you think Thuraya can be bought with gypsy gifts?*

Fawz   *I never gave her anything!*

Mullah   *You lie and you mince, you excite both men and women, you are a menace to decent habits and the stability of married life.*

Fawz   *What married life?*

Mullah   *Sex and procreation!*

The Representative of the Tourist Board has been subconsciously moving the metre rule in and out of his cupped palm, imitating the act of penetration. Realizing this, he stops momentarily and then resumes the action in an exaggerated manner, inviting the smutty laughter from some of the other envoys.

Fawz   *You filthy man!*

Speaker   *(To the audience.)* **Our colleague from the Tourist Board has tendencies.**

The Representative of the Tourist Board looks furiously at the Speaker, who has improvised at his expense.

Mullah   *If I see you again: it's this stick to your whippable, transvestite arse.*

Fawz   *What religion is yours?*

Mullah *Neither the delinquents', nor the cross-dressers'–*

Fawz *Do they have their own religions?*

Mullah *I am with the Organization, gelding.*

Fawz *I fear Allah and name his prophet as straight as the next man.*

Envoy *(Sings the call to prayer.)*

Mullah: *(Hearing the call to prayer.) I must make ablutions after you – (To the Speaker.) you are on my list.*

The Representative of the Tourist Board steps down from the raised platform.

Fawz: *What's this? A pearl. A giant pearl. Oh God, have I charmed you? The triangle is complete: My master loves Thuraya, I love my master and Thuraya loves me! It's diabolic, where in the folds of time can I hide this face? I have a life waiting for me that is a series of still images I can already see. Me in a wedding dress; me with my first child, me with my second child; me, stooped with my children grown tall around me, me dead. (As she speaks, she removes her latex lab gloves.) And there's another life waiting for me, I cannot see in any way, but I feel its circumference, dark and deep as a lake, at the edge of my fingertips.*

The Former Actress addresses the next lines to the Representative of the Council of Virtue and, in doing so, relays the revolutionary signal to him.

When water stands still it turns foul
And the arrow that does not leave the bow,
can never touch the target;
I am one who has always known
she will die young.

Bell announces end of scene.

Envoy Feylooti tells a joke.

Bell announces start of scene.

Feylooti   *A 90-year-old fella marries a 17-year-old lass. It's their*
wedding night and he says, 'Come on, then, love.' And she says,
'I don't know what to do, love.' And he says, 'Baaaaaa! She don't
know and I've right forgotten.'

Pre-recorded laughter from the 1963 audience combines with
the envoys genuine amusement at the joke. A wave of silliness
and chaotic, childlike energy washes across the laboratory.
The Representative of the Tourist Board taps his metre rule
emphatically on the steel laboratory table to restore order.

Speaker   *(Coyly to the audience.)* **Our colleague from the**
Tourist Board doesn't appreciate that type of humour – he
doesn't easily *rise* to the challenge himself.

The envoys giggle. The Representative of the Tourist Board
crosses the stage to confront the Speaker and, in crossing, notices
the Young Woman and the Representative of the Writers' Union
fumbling to hide something. He stops abruptly, moves towards
them, searches amongst the papers and props and finds the
Speaker's red notebook. He opens it, reads from it, then calmly
indicates to the Speaker to come towards him.

Speaker   *(To the audience.)* **Excuse me.**

The Representative of the Tourist Board marches the Speaker off
stage brusquely.

Scene Two, The Singing Leviathan

A wave of anxiety and nervous energy descends on the laboratory.
The Representative of the Writers' Union, inebriated, excited,
moves to the Speaker's podium.

Rep. Writers' Union   **This next scene – one of my favourites**
– saw it when I was eight. It is properly, truly filthy: beautiful!
Mr Lewis, bell, please.

The bell sounds. The envoys take their positions mechanically and
begin to deliver the lines.

Faris   *Here comes the fool, i' faith.*

Envoy   Nishami ululates.

The Young Woman obeys the instruction, without gusto.

Rep. Writers' Union   *(Wearily.)* **Mr Lewis, buzzer, please.**

A buzzer is sounded to stop the reconstruction. The envoys do not understand. The Representative of the Writers' Union moves towards them, swaying gently.

Rep. Writers' Union   What are you doing! Why do you think the costumes were brought in?! This scene is special! Its filth is real: in it, there's a man disguised as a woman! Get your togs on, and you *(To Young Woman.)* rub some lipstick on your smackers! *(To the audience.)* **My mother – bless her soul – used this scene to prove to us boys the dangers awaiting those who didn't wash their hands before supper, 'you'll end up like a bad lot, like Tagtiga and his pals in that terrible play'. No need to archive this.** *(He takes the Young Woman's headscarf.)* **Its place is carved in the heart.** *(He places the headscarf over the lens of the surveillance camera.)* Play it now, play it well – **bell!**

The bell announces the start of the scene. The stage picture, the colours of the lights, the brilliance of the costumes, all recall the Golden Age.[6] We are entering a new level of artifice in which the laboratory, momentarily, appears bearable. The sound of audience laughter from the 1960s is heard alongside the hiss of the historical recording.

Faris   *Here comes the fool, i' faith.*

Envoy   Nishami ululates.

The Young Woman ululates with relish. The Representative of the Council of Virtue enters, adorned in a sequin dress with wig, dark glasses, and with a white-gloved hand. He is dressed as the diva of 1960s Arab song, star of the East 'Kawkab al Sharq': Um Kalthoum.

Feylooti   *How now, my hearts! Did you never see the picture of a man in a dress?*

Tagtiga   *Welcome, ya Sitt.[7] Let's have a catch.*

Faris   *By my troth, the fool has an excellent breast. I had rather than 40 rupees I had such a leg, and so sweet a breath to sing, as the fool has.*

Feylooti   *My lady's hand is white. (He displays the revolutionary signal to the Former Actress.)*

Tagtiga   *Where are you going?*

Nishami   *To turn down the lights. (She steps off the platform to change her dress.)*

Feylooti   *Would you have a love song, or a song of good life?*

Nishami   *A love song, a love song!*

A vintage microphone descends from above and a follow spotlight encircles Feylooti. As the sound of violins starts the introduction to Um Kalthoum's 'Al Hobbi Ay' (What is Love), he begins to sing. The Former Actress stands, enamoured, on the edge of the circle of light. The Representative of the Writers' Union seizes the Young Woman and seats her affectionately on his lap. All accompany the song, as chorus.

Faisal Al Ameeri, Amal Omran. Photo by Mike
Ritter. *Feylooti: What is love?*

Rep. Writers' Union   You're laughing!

Young Woman   I can't help it.

Rep. Writers' Union   This was something else, this was something other, it was like, like … watching a revolution!

A loud noise interrupts the magic. Enter the Representative of the Tourist Board and the Speaker, holding a copy of Shakespeare's Twelfth Night *aloft. The Speaker has been physically abused.*

Speaker   *(In the language of the host venue.)* **I denounce myself.**

Rep. Tourist Board   In Arabic!

Speaker   *(In Arabic.)* I was the originator of the transgressive improvisation. I displayed wilful negligence in my duty towards the committee; I obscured the true origins of the 1963 play: an adaptation of William Shakespeare's *Twelfth Night*, written in 1601. I have conspired with this foreign source. In my defence, I say only that my real intention was to highlight the majestic historical transformation prophesied in the Shakespearean play that brought, 40 years after this play was written, the Puritans to power in England. The Puritans, keen protectors of civic health and their nation's standing in the world, enforced the closures of all theatres that harboured the 'sinful' entertainment. England became a great nation because of the Puritans. Many scholars, religious and otherwise, verify this. *(He signs the written confession, the Representative of the Tourist Board pockets it. Then, aside:)*

A plague upon sailors
The sea follows not a direction …

Rep. Writers' Union   *(Completing the verse.)* … rather, directions follow the sea.[8]

Speaker   *(To the envoys.)* Don't stop! You cannot stop!

The envoys resume the scene and song with renewed vigour; they dance and hop between the squares of the raised platform, marking the rhythm with their names: A3-B4-C6. To underline the requisite literalism – as he sees it – expected of the reconstruction, the Representative of the Tourist Board carries a stepladder onto the raised platform ensuring his character, the Mullah, is correctly positioned in the window of the upper floor of Thuraya's courtyard, which is projected on the screen.

Mullah   *Are you mad?! This is dancing, this is bending, this is transvestitism! Will blatant filth encroach on our beds and no man stir?*

Dead silence. The Representative of the Writers' Union, with a wave of his hand, makes the signal of the revolution.

Speaker   Witness: London, the 11th of February 1647.

On screen the portrait of Oliver Cromwell. The Representative of the Women's League enters dressed as a seventeenth-century English Puritan and reads, in English, from the act of the English Parliament.

Rep. Women's League   By ordinance of the present parliament: 'All Stage-players are hereby declared to be, and are, and shall be taken to be Rogues, and openly and publiquely whipt, Further, every person which shall be present and a Spectator at any such Stage-play, shall forfeit and pay the price of watching. Pay the price of watching!'

A flashlight photograph of the stage is taken from within the audience.

Speaker   *(To the audience.)* **We didn't ask you to turn off your mobile phones. I urge you to use them responsibly – bear witness.**

Rep. Tourist Board   Are you done? Where are your scripts? I command you to follow the text as written!

Rep. Council of Virtue   It's his line, not mine! *(Pointing towards the Representative of the Writers' Union.)*

Young Woman   *(Whispering the line, imploringly.)* We do stir and keep time, too!

Rep. Writers' Union   *(Unbuttoning his pants.)* Is this what you're looking for?

The Representative of the Tourist Board notices the headscarf that obscures the video camera and rushes to remove it.

Rep. Tourist Board   *(Holding up the headscarf.)* Whose is this?

Rep. Writers' Union   Mine.

The Representative of the Tourist Board smells the headscarf and fixes his gaze on the Young Woman.

Speaker   We are respecting the text!

Young Woman   *A flower, a flower for my master!*

The Representative of the Tourist Board lunges at her and stabs the metre rule into her lower abdomen.

Rep. Tourist Board   Dirty little whore! *(Raises the metre rule to strike her again. The Representative of the Student Union snatches it, the Former Actress points out the incorrectness of his position on the platform: he is outnumbered and has lost his metre rule.)* This hand will do more! *(Exits.)*

Nishami   *(In pain.) Sting me! Slap me! Burn me! I'll make you regret the day you first tasted your mother's milk.*

Rep. Writers' Union   *(Ruminating and eating peanuts, in Italian and French.)* Un idea magnifica! Une idée magnifique! *(Reading from the stage directions of the 1963 text.)* 'Scene Nine: In which the Lady's Maid, Nishami, makes a trap for the Mullah by forging a letter of unbridled fondness in her lady's hand, which she imitates well.'

Young Woman   *(Under her breath.)* Bastards.

Rep. Writers' Union   I'm thinking! I'm trying to promote tourism inside this Leviathan. *(To the Representative of the Womens' League.)* Comrade, sister?

Rep. Womens' League   Drunken poet.

Rep. Writers' Union   Could you be convinced to – how should I put it – whore for the cause?

Rep. Womens' League   Will you write my part?

Rep. Writers' Union   We'll all write it.

Rep. Tourist Board   *(Off.)* Representative of the National Student Union!

Summoned, the Representative of the National Student Union leaves the stage.

Rep. Council of Virtue   *(Nervous.)* Where's the palace?

Scene Three

The items of set from the Ruler's Palace, as seen in the archive film, are introduced. Though each item is tagged and labelled, in conformity with the rules of the reconstruction, the assembly of the palace is nonetheless theatrically impressive, almost operatic. The state is showing its strength, flexing its muscles; drapes fly in, a 1960s chandelier appears, a seat upholstered in zebra skin is carried on. The Representative of the Tourist Board oversees this, whipping stick in hand.

Speaker   Palace scene, palace scene, palace scene.

Bell announces the start of the reconstruction.

Ruler   *Have you learnt it, my little hawk?*

Fawz   *By heart.*

Ruler   *That is my text, my heart's constitution, the text by which she is the Ruler, I am the Ruled: go to her with that.*

Fawz   *I can't go again.*

Ruler   *Why not?*

Fawz   *She won't be won.*

Ruler   *Why not?*

Former Actress   I went to her with your 'text' and she received it like a knife to the womb.

The Representative of the Council of Virtue silently urges her not to improvise.

Ruler   *Fawz, are you in love?*

Fawz   *Yes!*

Ruler   *With Thuraya!*

Fawz   *No!*

Ruler   *Who then?*

Fawz   *One who's not even aware of my existence.*

Ruler   *Name her.*

Fawz   *I can't.*

Ruler   *Is she tall?*

Fawz   *About your height.*

Ruler   *Complexion?*

Fawz   *Not far from yours.*

Ruler   *Figure?*

Fawz   *Not unlike yours.*

Ruler   *Age?*

Fawz   *About yours.*

Ruler   *Veiled?*

Fawz   *In impossibility.*

Ruler   *Thighs like mine and my age? I know her – pluck her like a thorn from your heart!*

Former Actress   And you? Can you pluck the revolution[9] out of yours?

Ruler   *Thuraya is not part of my heart, she is central to my agenda!*

Fawz   *Must I go?*

Ruler   *As your name promises: to Victory!*

The Former Actress sings a couplet from Asmahan's 'Ya Raytni Tayr' (If only I were a bird). The Representative of the Tourist Board crosses to the Speaker's podium, removes the Speaker's suit jacket, ejects him from the podium and assumes the role of the Speaker.

Speaker   Be my guest.

Rep. Tourist Board   *(To the audience, in host language.)* **Hello, I speak only Arabic.** *(In Arabic.)* Good evening, gracious guests. The next few scenes form the crux of tonight's presentation. I'm in all of them. Through them, you will see how an upright, God-fearing citizen is seduced into animalistic desire, madness and extremism. The chaos and anarchy that follow are the direct results of a surfeit and excess of freedom. *(To the envoys.)* I remind you: treason is a poisoned sea, those that die in it are not to be mourned. I will give my all.

Speaker   *(In Arabic.)* And so will I – we spare no one. Rules of combat: full costume, direct address. You both, show me your hands!

The Representative of the Women's League and the Young Woman stand centre on the raised platform.

Young Woman   *(Wearing the white silk glove.)* My lady's hand is white.

The two women simultaneously display the revolutionary signal with their gloved hands.

Speaker   *(To the audience.)* **Beauty and depravity: more breeds more. Shield your eyes and open your hearts: freedom is a city with many points of entry.**

The Speaker turns all the available lighting sources in the direction of the audience, blinding them. Loud Qur'an verses, 56–58 of Surat al Anfal (The Spoils of War): 'Those of them with whom thou madest a treaty, and then at every opportunity they break their treaty, and they keep not duty (to Allah). If thou comest on them in the war, deal with them so as to strike fear in those who are behind them, that haply they may remember. And if thou fearest treachery from any folk, then throw back to them (their treaty) fairly. Lo! Allah loveth not the treacherous.'[10]

Scene Four

An Orange Grove, sublimely conceived.

Envoy   Enter Nishami. She lays the forged letter into the Mullah's path.

Nishami: A greased skewer.

Faris, Tagtiga and Nishami hide behind the orange trees.

Speaker   Enter the Mullah.

Mullah   O, to sire you now, Thuraya.

Tagtiga   (Aside.) There is a crime in me, waiting to leap out.

Mullah   It's not unknown, love knows not society.

Tagtiga   (Aside.) A crime in me that needs a knife.

Mullah   A morning like this morning, having been three months . married to Thuraya–

Tagtiga   (Aside.) They preach not what they do!

Mullah   I'd come from a day bed where I have left her sleeping–

Envoy   The Mullah sees the letter.

Mullah   What's this? (Reading the letter.) 'Signal to me, but do not speak in words; prattle and coo as do lovebirds.' A riddle!

Nishami   The rat rides the skewer.

Tagtiga   *Excellent woman.*

Rep. Writers' Union   *(To the Representative of the Student Union.) Sing us a song.*

He sings from 'Ya wardatan fi khayyali' (O rose in my imagination) by Farid Al Atrash. The atmosphere is reminiscent of an Egyptian silver screen classic from the 1950s. The voice reading the letter, in keeping with this aesthetic, dissolves into the voice of the beloved, Thuraya.

Mullah   *(Reading.) 'Your immutability has driven me to this confession. Lands have been liberated from their oppressors – so why not bodies, too? I've signalled my inclination towards you ceaselessly, but how slow and thick blooded you are.'*

Young Woman   *(Imitating Thuraya's voice.)* When will you learn the language of the other?

The Representative of the Tourist Board is startled, but resumes his reading eagerly.

Mullah   *Cast your chains of servility asunder, better be deemed ridiculous than be reviled, what others call madness is to me modernity; show yourself to me; be modern, be brave.*

Young Woman   *(Imitating Thuraya's voice.)* Speak in the language of power: in the language of the mind, in the language of lovers – speak English, Italian, Cantonese, French: show me the gift of your tongue.

Rep. Tourist Board   *(To the Speaker.)* That's improvised – but I like it!

Mullah   *(Reading.) 'Yours, One who dares to imagine and longs to see.'*

From this point onwards, it is no longer clear whether the Representative of the Tourist Board is speaking as the Mullah from the 1963 script, or as himself, improvising.

Rep. Tourist Board   She's ill and I am the cure: she's lost, and I'm her guide … Historical opportunity crossed with individual genius – *this* is how revolutions are made. Thuraya's breast in one hand, the keys to the state in the other: no contradiction anywhere. A dictionary! I need a dictionary!

Rep. Writers' Union   *(Offering his services, in Italian.) Sono io!*

Rep. Tourist Board   Ah, *sono io* – stay close, I'll be needing you.

Exit Representative of the Tourist Board.

Tagtiga   *(To Nishami.) I could marry you for this.*

Faris   *Me too.*

Rep. Tourist Board   *(Off.)* Envoys! Help me get dressed!

Nishami   *You called, Mullah darling?*

Exit Nishami.

Tagtiga   *Move! I've fallen in love!*

Rep. Council of Virtue   *(To the audience.)* **Sorry, sorry.** *(Addressing the surveillance camera, in Arabic.)* The text was altered, tampered with during the last scene. I have said what my duty and conscience dictate. That's it, thanks.

Enter Thuraya and Fawz, strolling in the orange grove.

Thuraya   *Do you know how to cast spells?*

Fawz   *On who?*

Thuraya   *Women.*

Fawz   *Women have a spell cast on them from birth.*

Thuraya   *Poor things!*

Fawz   *However hard a woman tries, she will always be the prey, never the predator.*

Thuraya   *Explain yourself.*

Fawz   *If they're pretty they're the prey of men, if they're ugly they're the prey of other women, and if they're clever they are their own worst enemy.*

Thuraya   *Then a woman can only be predator to another woman?*

Fawz   *That's correct.*

Thuraya   *Then explain this to me.*

Fawz   *What?*

Thuraya   *This! Here you are, a fully grown – to my eyes – man, in my garden and I have every intention of preying upon you!*

Fawz   *I am my master's servant.*

Thuraya   *Don't mention him again!*

Fawz   *My master intends to prey on you–*

Thuraya   *Answer my question and look at me! Yes, like that.*

Fawz   *You are exploiting the class difference between us. You are a lady: I am a servant. You are merely replicating the forms of male predation in the social sphere. In this garden you are the man, I am the woman.*

Thuraya   *Do you think it would matter to me if you were a woman? Don't answer.*

A recorded fanfare from the 1963 play announces the entry of the Mullah. The envoys involved in the 'plot' take up their positions in the laboratory-turned-orange grove.

Scene Five, the Fall – a glocal comedy

Enter the Representative of the Tourist Board as the Mullah. He is dressed in a loud, purple suit, orange tie, beardless, holding a hairdryer.

Mullah   *Thoo-Thoo?*

Thuraya   *Mullah Farhan!*

Mullah   *I beg you, Thoo-Thoo, call me Foo Foo. I want to show you my gifts!*

Thuraya   *What have you done to yourself?*

Mullah   *Broken them! The chains of servility cast asunder!*

Thuraya   *You look ridiculous.*

Mullah   *Better ridiculous than reviled!*

Thuraya   *Are you mad?*

Mullah   *What to others is madness is to me simply modern! I bring you signs.*

Thuraya   *What signs?*

Sticks out his tongue and wiggles it. One of the envoys signals to him not to improvise in this manner, but the Representative of the Tourist Board is cavalier and unconcerned.

Thuraya   *You seem not yourself.*

Mullah   *This is my new self!*

Thuraya   *Perhaps you should go to bed?*

Mullah   *To bed!*

The Representative of the Tourist Board, intent on seducing the Representative of the Women's League with his skills in foreign languages, consults with the Representative of the Writers' League and other envoys, repeating what is dictated to him in languages he does not comprehend. He derives a childlike thrill from this exercise, while the Representative of the Women's League duly incites him with lustful energy to go further in his linguistic odyssey.

Rep. Writers' Union   *(Whispering)* Si, si amore, facciamolo![11]

Rep. Tourist Board   *(To the Representative of the Women's League.)* Si, si amore, facciamolo!

The Representative of the Women's League responds to this improvisation with lusty glee.

Mullah   *I bring you a second sign.*

Thuraya   *Of what?*

Mullah   *My affection.*

Thuraya   *A hairdryer?*

Mullah   *Sechoir!*

Thuraya   *What for?*

Rep. Writers' Union   *(Whispering.)* C'est trop chic. J'adore les femmes aux têtes nues.[12] *(It's so chic. I love women with bare heads.)*

Rep. Tourist Board   *(To the Representative of the Women's League.)* C'est trop chic. J'adore les femmes aux têtes nues.

Thuraya   *Give it to Nishami.*

Rep. Students Union   *(Whispering.)* 将其插入[13]

Rep. Tourist Board*: (To the Speaker.)* Don't get too clever.

Young Woman   *(Whispering.)* Your love is oppression!

Rep. Tourist Board   Your love is oppression!

Young Woman   I cannot live under oppression!

Rep. Tourist Board   I cannot live under oppression!

Young Woman   I want to …

Rep. Tourist Board   I want to …

Young Woman   Defect!

Rep. Tourist Board   *(Suspicious, in Arabic.)* What is 'defect'?

The Representative of the Writers' Union clenches his fist and pulses the air, insinuating sexual intercourse.

Rep. Tourist Board   O!! *(Turns to the Representative of the Womens' League for confirmation. She mimes a second sexual act.)* No! *(Turns to the Young Woman for confirmation, who mimes a third, more explicit, sexual act.)* Ah! Thoo-Thoo: *(In English.)* **I want to defect! You, me de-fect! Me, you defect! Defect two times! Ten times! Defect, defect, DEFECT!**

The music stops. We hear the sound of a woman panting through a microphone. The Representative of the Writers' Union, armed with a clipboard, stands above the kneeling Representative of the Tourist Board, judge-like.

Rep. Writers' Union   To defect, a disertare al nemico, passer à l'ennemi?

Rep. Tourist Board   Yes, according to the path and sunna of the Prophet, Peace be upon Him!

Young Woman   A traitor and proud of it!

The sound of a heavy cage rolling is heard.

Rep. Writers' Union   You made a public plea for political asylum in a foreign city. You are an agent of the enemies of the state.

Rep. Tourist Board   *(Realizing, then to the surveillance camera.)* No, no, I was tricked. No!!

Speaker   Second Musical Interlude!

The Sound Technician plays a vinyl record – Andy Williams' 'Music to Watch Girls By' or 'Balghi Kull Mowaidi' by Mulhim Barakat and Georgette Sayigh – the envoys dance, throw confetti and lead the Representative of the Tourist Board, blindfolded, into the cage. As the cage door is slammed, the record needle slips and screeches.

Rep. Tourist Board   Rats!

Rep. Writers' Union   Fuck you!

Speaker   We continue the reconstruction of the decadent play! The next scene, blind fool on the seashore: prophecy of death.

Bell announces the start of the reconstruction. The Representative of the Council of Virtue as Feylooti the Blind Fool, strikes a sea drum and sings.

Feylooti   *Of what my eyes have seen, I sing:*

Birds of death fly hovering,
Mothers looking for their sons,
Sons begging for guns
To kill their fathers ...
Under the sand
The earth's black lungs
Exhale dragons.

The Counter Revolution: in which the laboratory seeks to
annihilate the rebel envoys. The lights cut out momentarily. A
weighted rope swings across the stage, knocking over a lab table.
A plug blows on the Sound Technician's desk, the Speaker's light
flickers. The smoke machine erupts. A lighting bar flies in above
the stage. The Speaker steps away from his position as a sandbag,
intended to assassinate him, falls where he had been standing. The
stage falls into darkness and the sound of more stage equipment
falling and collapsing is heard. Screams, distress, then silence.
The Representative of the Tourist Board, inside the cage, laughs
derisively.

Act Three, the Conclusions

The Deep State

Scene One

The sound of a generator brings the lights back up, reduced, altered. Sand falls in thin trails onto the destroyed posts of the laboratory.

Speaker   **Violence poisons the imagination** – *(To the Representative of the Tourist Board.)* you dog!

Rep. Tourist Board   The camera is filming everything!

Former Actress   I'll rip it out.

Speaker   Leave it. *(To the Representative of the Tourist Board, pulling him from the cage.)* You are in character, the text is perfectly intact, our commission runs through its phases, like a river beneath a city under siege. Into the torture scene – a truly Shakespearean moment! *(Throws him onto the raised platform.)*

The Young Woman enters with the Mullah's whipping stick and the hairdryer.

Nishami   *Peace unto the prisoners.*

Mullah   *Who's there?*

Nishami   *The People.*

Mullah   *My people!*

Nishami   *Who come to ogle at their oppressor and exact justice without pity.*

Mullah   *Women and foreigners have deceived us all; release me and all will be forgiven.*

Nishami   *Will you talk of nothing but women and foreigners!*

She beats him on his ankles with the stick.

Mullah   I deny all the charges in their entirety.

Young Woman   Will you deny: move to A4, leap to B6, crawl to D3. Will you deny 90 centimetres?

Rep. Tourist Board   She's improvising!

Young Woman   Can you deny stabbing a girl in the womb for offering you a flower!

Mullah   You are blinded by the lights of chaotic freedom, you are in a terrible darkness.

Nishami   You lie!

Mullah   You will create only darkness.

Nishami   YOU LIE!

She beats him with his stick and burns him with the hairdryer.

Nishami   Now I want to cut your ears and then your fingers and then your revolutionary organ.

Mullah   For every drop of my blood, I will poison a million children.

Nishami   Q. for question: what is the opinion of the fallen dictator towards his crimes?

Mullah   That his actions were a necessity to fight the forces of radical Islam and prevent sectarian civil war.

Nishami   Q. for question: what do you say of this?

Rep. Tourist Board   I say when the sand runs out, you will weep and beg for mercy when there is no mercy to be had.

She whips him hard, exhausts herself whipping. He lifts himself up from a broken position, a colossus rising, and removes the headscarf that was blindfolding him.

Nishami   (Hysterically.) Remain in darkness: the desert is thirsty for skulls like yours.

Mullah   (Mocking.) My people, my people, my people!

*The Representative of the Tourist Board collects his folders and
files from his station. The Young Woman, with her booted foot,
marks the rhythm of the chant 'Al Sha'ab Yurid Isqat Al Nidham' –
'The people demand the fall of the regime' – the signature slogan
of the Arab popular uprisings.*

Mullah   *I will be revenged upon the pack of you.*

Nishami: The people … who come to ogle at their
oppressor and exact justice without pity.
Fayez Kazak, Nowar Yousef. Photo by Rashid Al Bin Ali.

The Young Woman stops marking the rhythm of the chant. She lowers the zip of her boots and removes them. Picks up the headscarf, shakes it until it is straight, wraps it around her head and face leaving only her eyes exposed. She leaves the stage barefoot. The Representative of the Writers' Union moves onto the raised platform and retrieves the boots with great sadness.

Scene Two

The Representative of the Council of Virtue enters angrily, dressed in the full costume of the Ruler.

Rep. Student Union   Wrong costume, it's the Blind Fool scene now.

Rep. Council of Virtue   No more Blind Fool, the Blind Fool is no more! *(He rips a page from his script.)*

Speaker   *(Retrieving the page.)* By removing this page, you're inciting us to compose a new ending.

Rep. Council of Virtue   *(Defiantly holding his script.)* I dare you!

Speaker   *(To the Representative of the Writers' Union, slumped in a chair, fatigued.)* Please, don't tire now.

A bell announces the start of the scene.

Ruler   *This woman, your niece – Thuraya.*

Tagtiga   *Thuraya, yes.*

Ruler   *Is central to my agenda.*

Tagtiga   *Central.*

Ruler   *She is the text of our desire.*

Tagtiga   *Yes, the very text.*

Ruler   *Our desire is to place her name onto my tongue and pronounce it mine.*

Tagtiga   *Yours.*

Rep. Writers' Union   This text is seditious.

Rep. Council of Virtue   *(To the surveillance camera.)* I don't trust this man.

Rep. Writers' Union   *(Continuing in a whisper.)* It will give us no answers.

Speaker   It was written by an Englishman, five hundred years ago. We've come so far, we need to–

Rep. Council of Virtue   I don't ask questions.

Rep. Writers' Union   Let's continue.

Rep. Council of Virtue   B3! Move into B3!

Tagtiga   *My Lord, my master–*

Ruler   *Take this car.*

Tagtiga   *I take the car.*

Ruler   *Take this house.*

Tagtiga   *I take the house.*

Ruler   *Bring her to me! Make her succumb to my will.*

Tagtiga   *Thuraya, my niece, has ... how can I tell you ... she has shamed me, the family and the seat of Power.*

Ruler   *How?*

Tagtiga   *She's betrayed you to your messenger.*

Ruler   *My messenger?*

Tagtiga   *The Poet.*

Ruler   *The outsider?*

Tagtiga   *She loves Fawz ...*

Rep. Writers' Union   Do you know Fawz? Fawz that set her body alight in the square–

Ruler   *I have no knowledge of this.*

Rep. Writers' Union   Fawz that took a bullet to her heart and made a spring for millions to quench their thirst from–

Ruler   *I have no knowledge of this!*

Rep. Writers' Union   Who scribbles her name on school walls and chants it through a year of Fridays–

Ruler   *My love is as hungry as the sea! It digests as much.*

Rep. Writers' Union   Will your children drink seawater! Leave the women to their destinies, let them mouth the vowels of the sea.

Rep. Council of Virtue   I've not lost my respect for authority, you bastards!

Rep. Writers' Union   Pointless. My lord and master, fuck you too!

Rep. Council of Virtue   *(Furious.)* You – out! Out!

The Representative of the Writers' Union exits the stage.

Rep. Council of Virtue   *(To Former Actress.)* It's the last scene, get into position!

Former Actress   The last scene.

Rep. Council of Virtue   Bell!

The bell is sounded.

Ruler   *I thought you were too young but I see betrayal knows no age.*

Fawz   *Never!*

Ruler   *Tell me, how does she kiss?*

Fawz   *Impossible!*

Ruler   *Her lips, are they coy or wanton? I want to cut your balls off!*

Fawz   *I don't–*

Ruler   *Talk!*

Fawz   *I can't betray you.*

Ruler   *Palpably false!*

Fawz   *I love you.*

Ruler   *(Sings the schoolboy anthem mockingly.) 'God, my country, my ruler!'*

Fawz   *I'm not ... what I ... I'm not a man.*

Ruler   *You're a coward and a traitor!*

Fawz   *No ... I'm ... a woman.*

Ruler   *What did you say?*

Fawz   *My name is Fawzia.*

Ruler   *Prove it.*

Fawz undoes her male garments, releases her hair. She sings a love song. The Representative of the Council of Virtue raises his sleeve, shows his hand to the Speaker.

Rep. Council of Virtue   A new ending? I'll give you one. Now.

Speaker   I've waited for this moment for so many years.

The Representative of the Council of Virtue offers his hand to the Former Actress. She tries to take it in her own, he corrects her assumption and lays his hand gently on her throat; she accepts.

Ruler   *For your service done and since you called me master for so long, here is my hand. Men! Thuraya's prize is concluded: write this girl a cheque for 40 days' worth of oil; she sang the song I wanted to hear.*

Attendant   *Shall we record the song?*

Ruler   *I have no more need for music.*

The Representative of the Council of Virtue grips the Former Actress's throat and begins to strangle her. The Representative of the Women's League tries to undo his grasp.

Rep. Women's League   He's killing her! Help me!

Speaker   I can't move. I'm paralysed.

The Representative of the Student Union withdraws from the stage, terrified. The Representative of the Council of Virtue releases the Former Actress.

Rep. Council of Virtue   *(To the Speaker.)* I don't want Shakespeare, I don't want politics, I don't want theatre. No more art. I swear, by God, by my father, by my children, I swear, I have no more need for it. Each of you will be silent, silent as the grave. *(Removes the surveillance camera.)* You saw nothing. You heard nothing. Silent as the grave. Shh … Or I'll kill you, one by one, with a spade. *(Exits.)*

Pause. Silence.

Speaker   *(To the audience.)*

Since I was a boy, the night whispered in my ear:
I, the night, am your script and your director
I am your narrative and your scenes;
Without me you are hyenas devouring hyenas.
Since I was a boy, the day made a habit to bellow:
I, the day, am your light and your grid
I am your curtain and your stage;
Without me you are savages
Inheriting chaos.

Then, in the passage of a night and a day
All the picture frames fell apart
And inside the bellies of 18-year-olds that fear not death
History hoofed its horses
And in the teeth, fists and spit of the ruck
They held up a corpse and named it 'fear'.
'The fear has gone,' they said …
Fear, then, only fear's ghosts.

Farewell, I.
O happy, happy wreck:
Progress is done.

Exit Speaker, followed by the Sound Technician/Musician.

Scene Three

The light dies slowly across the duration of the scene.

Rep. Women's League   We're damned by words.

Pause.

Former Actress   Remember the scene I read to you?

Rep. Women's League   Which one?

Former Actress   The dream, the one the young writer brought, the cute one, you know the one, it doesn't matter, just try to remember, will you?

Rep. Women's League   Yes.

Former Actress   Say it, before the sand runs out.

Rep. Women's League   What for?

Former Actress   Just say it with me.

Pause.

Rep. Women's League   Tell me your name, without shame, without fear?

Former Actress   My name is Amal Omran.[14]

Rep. Women's League   Where are you from?

Former Actress   I'm from a village called Sadaf. I can't see you.

Rep. Women's League   Tell me your mother's name, without shame, without fear?

Former Actress   My mother's name was Fatima. Yours?

Rep. Women's League   Marianne. I can't see you.

Former Actress   Seeing's not everything. Describe the colour of your eyes without shame, without fear.

Rep. Women's League   My eyes are the colour of coffee with a drop of milk. Yours?

Former Actress   The colour of earth after rain.

Rep. Women's League   I can't see you.

Former Actress   Does it matter? Tell me what you do not know without shame, without fear?

Rep. Women's League   I'm ignorant of most things. But–

Former Actress   Have you tasted love? I'm drowning. I thought I could re-create myself, lose myself in the city …

Rep. Women's League   We will step out of this tower, beyond the line of the sun …

Former Actress   Live a hundred lives in the passage of a night.

Rep. Women's League   Past the men with patches on their eyes–

Former Actress   I thought life was an orchard of pomegranates–

Rep. Women's League   And wear our freedom like a new spring dress–

Former Actress   And time, a basket in my hand …

Rep. Women's League   It's material as thin as butterflies' wings … untouched by knives.

Pause.

Former Actress   *(Laughing suddenly.)* It's stupid – I have a stupid song in my head!

Rep. Women's League   *(Laughing with her.)* Sing it!

Former Actress   But how shall we live?

Rep. Women's League   I want to fly.

The sand falling from above runs empty. The darkness is entire.

End

Notes

1   The archive footage of this fictional performance is available for viewing at www.sabab.org.
2   See the following story board images for the performance of *The Speaker's Progress* directed by the author, drawings by Sam Collins:

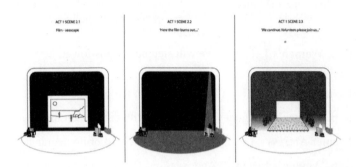

3   The play that forms the object of the reconstruction is a fictional 1963 Gulf Arab adaptation of Shakespeare's *Twelfth Night*. The main characters and storyline of Shakespeare's *Twelfth Night* are identifiable in this adaptation. For reference, as follows: The Ruler – Orsino; Thuraya – Olivia; Nishami – Mariah; Tagtiga – Toby Belch; Faris – Andrew Aguecheek; Mullah Farhan – Malvolio; Feylooti – Feste; Fawz – Viola.
4   Free translation of Abu Nawas's verse,

دَعْ عَنْكَ لَوْمِي فإِنَّ اللَّوْمَ إِغْرَاءُ, وَدَاوِنِي بِالَّتِي كَانَتْ هِيَ الدَّاءُ

5   Huriya: Arabic, meaning 'Freedom'.
6   The Golden Age of Arab Culture in the Twentieth Century refers to a period between the mid-1920s to the mid-1960s and varies from one country to another. This period combined the excitement of independence from colonial powers, the rise of the massively popular pan-Arab agenda of General Jamal Abdul Nasser in Egypt and the sense of new horizons opening before the people of the region. During this time, the region witnessed a distinct flourishing in the production of films, novels, music and theatre. One of the symbols of this era was the Egyptian singer, Um Kalthoum.
7   'Ya Sitt' – a pseudonym and term of reverence for Um Kalthoum.
8   Extract from Mudaffar Al Nawwab's poem, 'Arus al Saffa'in' (*The Queen of Ships*).

9   The line in Arabic puns on the name of Thuraya and the word for revolution, 'Thowra'.
10   Translated by Marmaduke Pickthall, *The Qur'an*, Everyman's Library.
11   Italian: 'Yes, yes, my darling! Let's do it!'
12   French : 'It's so chic. I love women with bare heads.'
13   Chinese: 'Plug it in!'
14   The name and birthplace of the Former Actress should be adapted to suit the name and birthplace of the performer playing the role.